The
Home Front

Seeing It Through - Arras and Passchendaele

David Bilton

Pen & Sword
MILITARY

First published in Great Britain in 2017 by
PEN & SWORD Military
an imprint of
Pen & Sword Books Ltd,
47 Church Street, Barnsley,
South Yorkshire.
S70 2AS

ISBN 978 1 47383 3 692

A CIP catalogue record for this book is available
from the British Library

Printed and bound in England by CPI Group (UK) Ltd, Croydon, CR0 4YY.

Pen & Sword Books Ltd incorporates the imprints of
Atlas, Archaeology, Aviation, Discovery, Family History, Fiction, History, Maritime, Military,
Military Classics, Politics, Select, Transport, True Crime, Air World, Frontline Publishing,
Leo Cooper, Remember When, Seaforth Publishing, The Praetorian Press, Wharncliffe
Local History, Wharncliffe Transport, Wharncliffe True Crime and White Owl.
For a complete list of Pen & Sword titles please contact:
Pen & Sword Books limited

47 Church Street, Barnsley, South Yorkshire, S70 2AS, England.
E-mail: enquiries@pen-and-sword.co.uk
Website: www.pen-and-sword.co.uk

Contents

Acknowledgements

As with my previous books, a great big thank you to the staff of the Prince Consort's Library and Reading Central Library for their help, kindness and knowledge during the pre-writing stages of this book. Once again, the text has been checked and corrected by Anne Coulson – thank you very much.

While some of the pictures come from books mentioned in the bibliography, many are from my own collection.

Introduction

This book is the fourth volume in a series that illustrates life on the Home Front during each year of the First World War. The many photographs show life through the eyes of those not on the military frontline. The book portrays the life of ordinary citizens and how they experienced the war. 'Important' people appear only as part of the context of everyday life.

This book is not solely about Britain. Though the major part of it does record British life, I have attempted to show the international commonality of various themes through illustrations from other countries both Allied and enemy. Readers may be familiar with some of the images, but most have not been published since the war, and others have never been published. As the photographs form the main focus of the book, I have quoted liberally from my previous books on the Home Front to provide the historical context, using the experiences of Hull and Reading as typical and also as contrast. While the photos, where possible, show an international theme, the majority of the following text concerns Britain during the period, with some French and German comparisons.

It is not chronological and, although themed, topics do cross over. Similarly, the difference between being in the forces and being on the Home Front can seem a grey area. It took a long time to train new recruits, and that training was done on the Home Front. In many areas, there were more people in uniform than out of it, a fact that became accepted as part of life.

What was 'The Home Front'? There are many interpretations of the phrase: 'the sphere of civilian activity in war'; 'the civilian sector of a nation at war when its armed forces are in combat abroad'; 'the name given to the part of war that was not actively involved in the fighting but which was vital to it'; an 'informal term for the civilian populace of the nation at war as an active support system of their military. Military forces depend on "home front" civilian support services such as factories that build materiel to support the military front'; it 'refers to life in Britain during the war itself'. All of these have elements of truth but none fully describe the range of experiences that shaped the Home Front.

If this book is about life away from the combat zone, then some of what happened on the Home Front cannot be recorded here. For those caught in a Zeppelin raid, the Home Front became a war zone; it was not always 'All quiet on the Home Front' as assumed by the title of one oral history book. In this and the following volumes, I define the Home Front as the totality of the experience of the civilian population in a country affected, directly or indirectly, by the war. As there were considerable numbers of military personnel on the Home Front, interacting with the civilian population, they too are included.

This again needs some examination. The Home Front was not a singular experience. Life in the countryside was different to that in the town or city, the latter being more quickly affected by change. Life in the Scottish Isles differed from life in the Kent countryside. Again, life in a coastal town on the east of the country was unlike that on the west. Of course the whole country experienced some basic similarities but there were many factors that varied the war's effects. How could a family who lost their only son experience the same war as a neighbour with five serving sons who all returned? What similarities were there between the family of a conscientious objector and one whose father/husband had been killed, or between an Irish family and a Welsh one?

While there is a common link between all of these examples, what links can be found between Belgian, French, Dutch, German, Japanese or Russian families? All these countries had a Home Front and all were directly affected by the war. There are some obvious differences. Neutral Holland was quickly affected by the war on its borders, and Japan, an isolated Allied power, fought in the Pacific and escorted convoys to Europe but was otherwise largely unaffected. Both were unlike the other countries which, despite some differences, were all united by an invasion, long or short, of their Home Fronts.

We can add further layers to the civilian experience of the war through the Home Front. Neutral countries had to defend themselves against possible aggression and were on a war footing, factors which inevitably affected civilian life. They were not at war, so nationals of the warring countries were free to move about as before the war and spying was rife. As safe havens, they became the guardians of hundreds of refugees or prisoners of war. And, as in the warring countries, commodities became short because, once at sea, their ships became targets.

Combatant countries on the continent experienced two types of Home Front, the obvious one being the civilians behind the fighting front. But in an occupied country civilians were behind both sides of the line. All shared the same nationality, but lived on the Home Front, very differently, enduring different constraints.

This book therefore illustrates life on the Home Front for civilians on both sides of the wire. It is impossible to look at every aspect of life, so I have selected themes that seemed to dominate the year.

GWI-HF_1 What nationality is this nurse?

GWI-HF_2 What nationality is
this nurse? Is there a hidden
text from the images?

GWI-HF_3 A postcard issued by a tobacco company expressing what everyone wanted. Welcoming the New Year and with it victory.

The Home Fronts in 1917

So long, so far

In the twenty-nine months since the war had started, much had changed, and over the next twelve months there would be further change: change would be the only constant. The change to a war footing would be intensified as the Home Front became involved in what would become a 'total war'. As even more industries switched to war production, there would be further shortages. Goods would be in short supply because of the urgent need for ever-increasing quantities of munitions.

The constant demand by the army for more men to replace those in the ever-lengthening casualty lists meant that many in what had been reserved occupations would suddenly find themselves being 'called up'. A shortage of men was countered by increased employment for women and a further dilution of labour. Women continued to face hardship and danger in their work. During 1917, 189 munitionettes were diagnosed with toxic jaundice: 44 cases were fatal. And there were explosions in munitions factories, the most famous of which occurred at Silvertown less than three weeks into the New Year.

This mass mobilisation of the female workforce had had some benefits. It gave many working-class women independence. In the factories wages were high (though naturally not as high as men's). The higher wages gave women money to spend on things previously only dreamt about, furs, fancy night-gowns, make-up, powder and silk stockings. Skirts became shorter, trousers were worn and many felt able to smoke in public. In contrast to this, it was now the fashion for middle-class women to dress plainly. For many of the wealthy the war brought little change; they attended the fashionable events dressed as they had been before the war. The changes and relative lack of danger at home caused a gap to develop between the Home Front and the men fighting at the front, who felt like strangers when they came home on leave.

The government provided crèches so women could work, pregnant workers were catered for, night work was forbidden to those under 18 and regular food was provided in special canteens. The latter was important as, in all the warring nations, and in many neutral countries, one of the biggest issues of 1917 would be food.

Of the warring nations, Germany faced the worst food problems. While the Allies could count on food from overseas (although much was lost to submarine activity), Germany could not. As a result, at the start of the year most foods were rationed and those not were difficult to get hold of. Many foods were now made from replacements. With little real coffee available, an ersatz coffee was manufactured from acorns, chicory, herbs and berries or roasted barley. Milk was powdered.

The list grew as one foodstuff after another became increasingly hard to find. Naturally, the black market flourished. Britain and France had still not introduced rationing but shortages were becoming more common and could only get worse as the war continued.

1916 drew to a close, no-one mourning its end. Nevertheless no-one was aware of the true scale of what the New Year would bring. It would be costlier and more expensive than they imagined as they saw the New Year in with their watered-down beer. Predicted shortages would become real, even more money would be needed to win the war, and, once again, the war would not be over by Christmas. The strain the British population were under is evidenced by a comment from a solicitor, employed by a cigarette manufacturer, given in the City of London Court: 'There are more cigarettes being smoked now than ever.'

In Reading, typical of the many small towns across the country, there was little to mark the coming of the New Year. It was the same in London where only a few lingered in the drizzling rain for the hour when night becomes morning. In Hull, most people stayed home. With restaurants closed, and no bells to chime, there was little point in being out. 'A year of abounding hope could not have been ushered in more quietly or more soberly.'

The Reading and Hull newspapers saw the New Year differently. Reading papers ignored it, with only a parish church magazine seeing fit to comment. The Reverend Canon Fowler, at St Peter's Church in Earley, expressed his feelings about 1917: 'A New Year is just opening upon us. It may well be one of the most important years in our nation's history; may God bring us safely through it.' However, in Hull, *The Eastern Daily News* was more loquacious, but sombre in its first editorial of the New Year: 'What a contrast to the ringing out of the Old and the ringing in of the New before the war cast its broad shadow of sorrow and bereavement over the world! The old year slipped away quietly, and 1917 came in just as quietly. True a few folk kept up the old custom of waiting in the city square until the New Year was born, but it was a small crowd, and as quiet as it was small. No sirens screeched, no bells rang out, there was no booming of the fateful hour which marked the dividing line between the Old and the New…And so 1916 passed away with few regrets save for those who have gone with it, and 1917 was born with great expectation and hope.'

A journalist for the Hull Daily Mail recorded his thoughts on the first day of the New Year in the 1 January 1917 edition: 'On this New Year morning there is some blue in the sky; great events also mark the birth of 1917…Today a great number of Englishmen are called up to the colours to take their part in our defence…The way women have come to the rescue is more noticeable now…The increase in fares on railway trains, beginning today, will tend to reduce unnecessary travelling, though it will inconvenience those who need to make journeys.' Although heavily used by the military, trains had managed to continue to provide a high level of service to the ordinary traveller but this could only last as long as the French government could provide sufficient locomotives for the British Army's needs as well as its own. When the French government wanted the return of more than 600 of them, the only source from which they could be replaced was Britain. As well as trains, the army needed rails and coal. There was a limited supply of everything, so, to mitigate the shortages, services vanished or were curtailed and many reduced in speed with many stations being closed. When no extra trains were put on for Easter and the operators would only sell tickets to the capacity of each train, it was a sure signal that there would be tough travel times ahead.

The railway problem was not unique to Britain. In Italy the railways relied on British coal, the deliveries of which fell short of requirements. To help, in return for the loan of eleven Italian destroyers for convoy escort duty, Britain agreed to send 700,000 tons of coal, including some from America. By the end of November the national stock stood at 350,000 tons. As a consequence the railways ran slowly and often not at all.

On a more mundane level, one writer noted that 'the increase of hair-cutting and shaving prices is another indication of the New Year.'

In France, President Poincaré was to describe 1917 as the year of confusion. There were no new plans to break the trench deadlock, and at home the war was now part of life. German peace moves were rejected as were those from Austria and from the Pope. On both sides it was war to the end, whatever the cost. What was impossible to predict was the collapse of the Russian Empire, a boon to the German forces, and as a replacement, the entry of America into the war, a boon to the Allied armies. While the two can be seen to cancel each other out, as the Americans would not arrive in force before 1918, the Russian collapse had a marked effect on French Home Front morale, 'encouraging and fomenting pacifist-defeatist agitation'. The Russian collapse would have far-reaching effects in 1918 and result in the long-hoped-for end to the war.

American entry into the war meant more than men and equipment. It meant increased shipping that would bring with the armaments vast quantities of sorely needed food for the Allies. It would also increase the protection for British convoys.

With the rapidly changing situation in Russia, many British investors would lose their money when the Romanoff dynasty fell: the new government felt no responsibility for the country's debt. However, with the reduction in fighting on the Eastern Front, there was less need to send munitions, so more could be sent to other fronts.

Change also meant control. In Britain this was achieved by additions and extensions to DORA (the Defence of the Realm Act). Many apparently harmless actions became potentially serious offences. Apart from prohibitions against careless talk, there were scores of 'don'ts' which separately seemed silly but which added up to a necessary code of safeguards for the protection and promotion of the war effort. A civilian could not send abroad any letter written in invisible ink, trespass on railways or loiter near railway arches, bridges or tunnels. Purchasing binoculars required official authorisation; it was forbidden to fly any kite that could be used for signalling, buy whisky or other spirits on Saturday or Sunday, or any other day except between noon and 12.30 pm. Paying for any intoxicating liquor for another person, except as a host of that person, at lunch, dinner or supper was prohibited, as was giving bread to any dog, poultry, horse or any other animal. A more obviously sensible rule restricted the entry of civilians into special military areas around the coasts.

By far the most pressing shortage was that of food. It was not a simple case of there being insufficient food. In Britain, some of the problem had to do with price. Well-stocked butchers in London were charging prices 250 percent higher than before the war. By the end of the year bloaters had reached 6d each. Price rises caused the most hardship to those with fixed incomes (the rentier class) but those with higher incomes were not always at an advantage. Some commodities remained hard to obtain, like butter and sugar. Even margarine proved difficult to get in some areas and queues became the norm. Sugar supply was a major grievance and many areas were quick to introduce their own system of rationing, which was followed at the start of 1918 by a national scheme which came only after a succession of ugly demonstrations and industrial threats, mostly in the winter of 1917-18, when people queued to receive nothing.

The lack of sugar hit the consumer in a range of ways: sugar scarcity restricted brewers, grocers and sweet manufacturers. In January sweet and chocolate production was reduced and beer production fell to half that of 1914. Jam making became impossible, causing the wastage of large quantities of fruit, and 'sugar days' attracted large queues outside grocers' shops. Substitutes for ordinary sugar included syrup made from sugar beet, honey sugar, glucose and generic products quaintly named as 'Consip' and 'Sypgar'. When the sugar bowl disappeared from the tables of Lyons cafés (instead a bowl was carried from table to table), it was obvious there was a severe shortage. By April there was less than ten days' supply available in the country. The Ministry of Food met hostility from the temperance movement when it was suggested that sugar was better utilised in beer production.

Coupled with the sugar shortage there was a lack of many of the raw materials needed for beer production. With production reduced by government order, 'pubs' were rationed and, when sold out, stocks could not be replaced until the next week. A decrease in sales meant a comparable decrease in profits so price rises were inevitable. When prices rose to 8d a pint in Liverpool, dockers wrecked some pubs and boycotted others, forcing the government to increase beer production by a third. As in America, there was a strong temperance element that tried to get the government to ban alcohol during and after the war. The movement had the support of the Bishop of London and Harry Lauder, the popular entertainer. Fortunately for morale, the idea was not adopted.

There was no shortage of game. 'The absence of sportsmen from their estates and the consequent diminution of shooting parties' had the effect of increasing the number of pheasants and partridges which for two years had been left largely unmolested. Complaints appeared in the daily papers concerning the 'ravages of the birds in the fields and gardens in many parts of England,' and it was suggested that there should be a relaxation of the Game Laws. Writing in 1917, Reverend Reeve complained about the problem in his home area of Stondon Massey, Essex: 'We have been sufferers in this neighbourhood from the overstock of game. The Rectory Garden has been constantly visited by pheasants from the adjoining woods, and early and late they have battened upon our green-stuff. Nearly every form of green vegetable has been stripped to the stalk, and this is when we are being urged to make every yard of ground profitable!'

Some foodstuffs were difficult to find only at certain times of the year; an example is the supply of potatoes, scarce up till the arrival of the new crop in the summer of 1917, but thereafter, due to a good harvest, plentiful, but at a price.

By the end of the year, queues (a new word in the English language) had reached epidemic proportions with shortages in a whole range of everyday foodstuffs like meat and tea. One queue, reported *The Times* on 10 December, for margarine, in Walworth Road, London, was estimated to consist of 3,000 people and after 2 hours of sales 1,000 went away empty-handed. To make sure of supplies on Saturday mornings, women started to queue at 5am, babes in arms and children at their skirts. The queuing was not just confined to the final purchaser; by the end of the year butchers were queueing to make sure they got their supplies to sell to the public.

Food was still available and there was no danger of anything vaguely resembling famine, as there was in parts of central Europe. Foods then classed as exotic dishes, like tinned fish, were readily obtainable, although few would eat them. There was no shortage of bread; its price was the same as a year previously and indeed decreased later in the year through governmental control of prices. With changing government directives though, its quality had slowly diminished as various other substances had been added like potato flour, wheat husk and other cereals. The population wanted white bread and this, for a while, bakers had tried, under these circumstances, to provide, but by the end of 1917 it was no longer possible. Even with all the complaints about its unpalatability more bread was being consumed than ever before, even than in pre-war days.

The use of other cereals meant that there was less food available for animal use, which in turn reduced the availability of pork, bacon and other meats, and eggs. The police were even given the task of taking an inventory of livestock to prevent the unnecessary consumption by animals of grain fit for human consumption.

The available food was not being distributed fairly and in many areas shops were stormed to force shopkeepers to release their commodities. There was now an urgent need for the government to provide everybody with an equal supply of whatever foodstuffs were available.

Earlier restrictions under DORA had made reference to bread and animals: picking up bread crusts thrown away by navvies constructing a new aerodrome and then feeding them to his pigs resulted in a £50 fine for a farmer. A rigid interpretation of the law meant that many people were punished for perfectly understandable things like giving meat to a dog (£20 fine) or leaving a loaf on a shelf in a cottage from which the worker was moving (£2 fine) or, after running out of cattle-cake, feeding the cattle with bread so they did not die (three months in jail). The year also produced regulations that attempted to stop food hoarding; the authorities could enter any premises thought to contain more food than was required for normal consumption. The government also prosecuted anyone selling above the maximum price; fines were high, with one potato farmer being fined £5,500 plus costs. With bread waste estimated at 10,000 tons a week, there was a real danger of supplies not lasting until the next harvest. The government was also strict on shopkeepers, who were not allowed to turn away non-regular customers or charge what they thought the market would bear.

A major reason for the food shortage was the U-boat campaign. During the last four months of 1916, 632,000 tons of shipping had been sunk and the President of the Board of Trade had reported that a complete breakdown in shipping would come before June 1917. On 1 February, the Germans declared unrestricted warfare on all merchant ships arriving and leaving Allied ports.

In March, towards what became known as the 'turnip winter', general food prospects were so unsure that arrangements were made to set up communal kitchens, and, soon after, the first one was opened in Westminster Bridge Road by the Queen. Fortunately the decrease in shipping losses obviated the need for the kitchens. However, a lot of food had been lost to the U-boat campaign; between January and June 1917, 47,000 tonnes of meat and 87,000 tonnes of sugar were lost. The introduction of the convoy system in May eventually cut ship losses and improved the food situation so that there was no longer a chance of the country being defeated by starvation.

British merchant vessels lost by enemy action

Year	Ships lost	Lives lost	Gross tonnage
1914	64	69	241,201
1915	278	2,371	855,721
1916	396	1,217	1,237,634
1917	1,197	6,408	3,729,785

British merchant vessels lost by enemy action in 1917

Year	Ships lost	Lives lost	Gross tonnage
January	49	276	153,666
February	105	402	313,486
March	127	699	353,478
April	169	1,125	545,282
May	122	591	352,289
(convoys)	122	416	417,925
June	99	468	364,858
July	91	462	329,810

Year	Ships lost	Lives lost	Gross tonnage
August	78	356	196,212
September	86	608	276,132
October	64	420	173,560
November	85	585	253,087
December			
Total	1,197	6,408	3,729,785

The Food Controller, Lord Devonport, launched a voluntary rationing scheme. Cancelling the order to limit the number of courses for lunch or dinner in a hotel or restaurant, he asked consumers to limit themselves to 4lb of bread a week, 2½lb. of meat and 4 ounces of sugar. Further impositions in hotels and restaurants were two potato-less days a week and one meatless day; also banned were afternoon teas that cost more than sixpence. The voluntary imposition was 'Eat less bread and victory is secure'. One eminent expert on nutrition told audiences nationwide that they did not need to eat so much, that beer was good for them and that they should have a coffee before going out in the cold: not tea because it contained an oil that dilated blood vessels. For those who liked their beer his words were especially welcome; not only did it contain minerals, vitamins, sugars and 'proteids' but it 'was as good as milk for energy, and its manufacture created by-products that could be used for animal foodstuffs and in foods such as compressed soup squares'.

In order to aid the voluntary economy campaign, the King and Queen adopted the voluntary scale of national rations in February and in May a Royal Proclamation was read out across the country on four consecutive Sundays. It was simply a call to eat less bread in order to defeat the Germans, and not to waste grain on horses unless it was to maintain the breed in the national interest. Bread economy worked and by the end of May consumption was down by 10 per cent. To assist, the Northcliffe press suggested that the rich should consume luxury items that the poor could not afford or found unpalatable.

While it was felt it would be difficult for the working classes to reduce bread consumption, it was the same for everyone. Bread was an essential: putting it on the sideboard, rather than the table, helped reduce consumption. For those accustomed to muffins, tea cakes, light pastries and sugar bowls in restaurants it was a taxing time. A price restriction between 3pm and 6pm, unless the food contained meat, fish or eggs, and a further restriction limiting bread, biscuit and cake to just two ounces, hit the middle classes. To further reinforce the message, the public was urged to 'Eat Slowly – You Will Need Less Food.' A further emphasis was placed upon shipping space that told the public that the weekly wastage of bread was equivalent to nine shiploads. Bread consumption was a serious matter and bakers were fined for selling under-weight loaves and for selling it under twelve hours after baking: an East End baker was sentenced to 21 days for just such an offence.

In June, Lord Rhondda was appointed as Food Controller and rapidly imposed stricter controls: throwing rice at weddings was forbidden, feeding pigeons in London or stray dogs anywhere was made illegal, potato flour was to be added to bread to reduce wheat consumption and, along with the match seller and bootlace vendor, the muffin man also disappeared. Tramps had also all but vanished from the streets.

Any future shortage of wheat flour could be blamed on a shortage of shipping and the U-boat campaign. As a countermeasure to the predicted shortfall of production in North America, the government bought three million tons of wheat, at a cost of £26,600,000, from Australia. When the expected shortage did not materialise, it chose to leave it in Australia because of the extra shipping requirements. 'The British Government…was content to leave the wheat to rot because at least it was not taking up valuable shipping space.'

Food shortages were to some extent ameliorated by the great patriotic allotment campaign that got under way during the year. By May of 1917 it was estimated that there were half a million allotments and vegetable plots under cultivation. Tennis clubs dug up their courts while private gardens dug up their flowerbeds. Everywhere people grew vegetables and even the King and the Prime Minister took part. The Archbishop of Canterbury sanctioned Sunday labour and services were held on allotments, while tea on the allotment became a normal Sunday event. Those too lazy to garden simply stole, resulting in allotment guards and the introduction of severe penalties for thefts – £100 fine or six months in prison.

In order to increase home production, a further scheme was introduced by the Board of Agriculture. A special food production department was set up in January, with the telegraphic address 'Growmore', whose remit was to increase Britain's food-growing capacity to a maximum, creating a country free from food imports. To do this required three million extra acres under cultivation and a massive increase in the agricultural workforce. The shortfall in workers on the land was quickly addressed by the introduction of the voluntary Women's Land Army. Further assistance was provided by the use of prisoners of war and soldiers who were released as and when needed; many were in training, stationed at local camps or recuperating wounded. And at harvest time there were many holidaymakers who were happy to be involved.

By 1918 the amount of land under cultivation had risen from 5.2 million (nearly 13 million acres) to 6.4 million hectares (nearly 16 million acres). The target for cultivation had been met.

Even though vegetables were never rationed, and many tens of thousands of people were now growing their own, it was still necessary to supplement the diet with extras provided by nature like dandelion leaves instead of lettuce – and of course there was never a shortage of nettles: 'One thing we used to eat – and it was surprising how nice they were – were boiled nettles. They were nice as a vegetable.' The government also recommended them in a food economy pamphlet:

Stewed Nettles.

Wash the nettles, and put them into boiling salted water, and boil until they are nearly done. Strain off the water, put in two teaspoonfuls of milk and a heaped teaspoonful of butter or margarine, and stir briskly till boiling point is reached.

   Another way of serving nettles is to cook them in fast-boiling water until tender, drain them carefully, and press into a pie-dish. Sprinkle over a few crumbs, seasoning to taste, and a little grated cheese, with a few tiny pieces of butter. Place in a brisk oven for a few minutes.

Other foods were also collected from the hedgerows. Reverend Reeve recorded in his diary for 27 September: 'School children are everywhere employed gathering the blackberries in School Hours under the control of their Teachers. The fruit is packed in baskets provided of regulation size, and sent by rail to the Army jam factories, while cheques are sent to the Teachers and payment authorized to the children of threepence per pound.'

   In contrast to the privations of the many, for those with money food was not an issue. *Herald* reporter, Francis Meynell, contrasted the sixpenny meal offered at a food kitchen that was thought to be good value with one in the West End. Under the headline, 'HOW THEY STARVE AT THE RITZ', the meal 'consisted of hors d'oeuvres, "a rich soup", sole and lobster, chicken (half a bird per person), three rashers of bacon and three tomatoes, fruit salad and coffee.' They demanded cream for the soup, the fish and the fruit. It flowed freely and was also provided for the coffee. There was no shortage of bread. On leaving the restaurant he was greeted with 'three old women huddled up in their rags for the night'.

   The Lord Mayor's Banquet went ahead despite opposition; a menu that consisted of clear soup, fillets of sole, casserole of partridge, roast beef and sweets, washed down with punch, champagne and port made little concession to the food shortages felt across the country. In ordinary homes the food was considerably blander than this as shortages of sugar, tea, butter and bacon made themselves felt. A December day's menu in a typical suburban home was uninspiring. Breakfast might include porridge (without milk or sugar), tea with milk and sugar, and potatoes fried in fat, lunch might consist of meat (salt brisket) and two vegetables (generally carrots and potatoes), milk pudding and cheese, tea would consist of bread and jam, while supper was maize semolina.

   Not every child remained in school. Thousands were given permission to leave school underage to help in the factories and on the land. During the year Herbert Fisher, President of the Board of Education, travelled the country looking at schools. Taking into account the needs of the country in the future and looking at the number of men who were unable to fulfil the army's needs, he drafted a new scheme of education. In August, he proposed to provide nursery schools, check child labour – even though it had helped the nation during the war – establish compulsory part-time day continuation schools up to the age of 18, extend the school medical service to ensure the physical fitness of all children and young persons and raise the leaving age to 14. The Act was passed in 1918 but later watered down due to financial stringency.

France was beset by the same food shortages. Sugar was rationed and long lines waited outside grocery stores for their quota. 'As other shortages appeared, similar lines would wait for milk, chocolate and potatoes.' Like London, Parisians with money could still enjoy the high life. 'From the Madeleine to the Place de la République, Paris was…a scene of "tremendous gluttony". The restaurants, ablaze with light behind their heavy blinds, were crowded with diners.'

Sugar was the first serious shortage, particularly in the Paris region where tea shops and sweet shops were closed two days a week, and in restaurants a customer could only have ten grammes. Again, as in Britain, restaurant fare was limited. Customers could only purchase a two-course meal, including only one of meat and with less choice to reduce waste. No subsidiary dishes were permitted and the diner was offered the choice of two from the two soups and nine dishes allowed, but of course this could be supplemented by second helpings.

The waste of bread was also an important issue. As in Britain, war bread, mixed with a range of other materials was unpopular, but, unlike in Britain, it was of such poor quality that much was left at the table. To make matters worse, fancy bread was prohibited, cakes for cafés limited, biscuit production reduced and patisserie forbidden for two days a week. Then in May came meatless days – a problem solved by buying, when available, and if well-off enough, two days' supply.

There were other shortages to contend with. The loss of France's coalfields to the Germans and the call-up of many younger miners in Britain naturally led to a coal shortage. In April there was a shortage of coal in London, which by the onset of autumn had not been solved. Indeed it had been made worse by the amount of money that the working classes were now earning and the fact that rationing entitled them to it. The shortage was more acute in France as its coal came from Britain.

The winter of 1916/17 was extremely cold, with temperatures in Paris falling to -7°C. Pipes froze and shop windows frosted. The shortage of coal meant that most were cold. People queued for hours often to go away empty-handed, coal-carts were besieged and their loads shared out, paid for by the honest citizens. Fuel was so short that the Jardin d'Acclimatisation, famous for its tropical flora, was left unheated: the plants perished. People of all classes, if they could not afford to have someone do it for them, pushed prams around the city looking for wood or coal for the fire. There was also a scarcity of candles and lamp-oil.

In Germany, the winter of 1916/17 really was a turnip winter. 'Everything that made life tolerable was becoming desperately short – adequate clothing, heating, food.' Fortunately there were turnips to eat. People were gaunt and bony, and, recorded Princess Blücher, 'growing thinner every day'. In February she recorded seeing 'faces like masks, blue with cold and drawn with hunger, with the harassed expression common to all those who are continually speculating as to the possibility of another meal.' Food was far scarcer than in Britain or France, and it was also proportionately more expensive. While wages had risen 15 per cent, prices were on average up 67 per cent. Fat people were uncommon and regarded with suspicion.

Such was the seriousness of the impending food crisis for Germany that one writer felt that the 'drama of the battlefield' had changed to the 'drama of the larder'. As proof, in January, on two occasions, angry Berliners stormed the city's food markets. While British and French customers had cuts of meat to choose from, German butchers' shops were displaying crows. In the countryside in Britain and France, food was still available, while in Germany food was smuggled across the border to get foreign currency or hoarded for private use. The police searched farms and the slaughter of your own pig meant being deprived of your meat ticket for weeks. However, a thriving black market was available for those with money.

Meat consumption was a quarter of that pre-war. Milk was scarce and social workers had to make sure that children had their fair share. Some shortages were genuine, others created by bureaucratic short-sightedness. After a violent wave of protest in April, after the bread allowance was cut, again, the authorities promised more meat. Ignoring the farmers, they ordered all milking cows in certain districts to be slaughtered to provide the meat. There was then a glut of meat, some of which was thrown away, and an even greater shortage of milk.

Food shortages were further exacerbated by the poor state of the railways. Trains moved so slowly that, in the severe winter, perishable goods froze and were useless. Farmers similarly had transport problems getting their produce to the railway. The untended roads were potholed and waterlogged when it rained and, to make the journey even slower, few horses were available to pull the carts. Undermanned farms relied on inexperienced PoW workers, where they were available, and equipment went rusty.

German war bread, Kriegsbrot, had been in existence for some time and, like its Allied counterparts, was made from a mixture of ingredients and not highly regarded. As the war progressed, it was further diluted and by 1917 Princess Blücher noted that it was being stretched 'with some of those numerous subterranean vegetables coming under the rubric of the turnip, of whose existence we never dreamed before.'

To ease the food situation, mobile war kitchens were introduced. In Britain the war kitchens were stationary, giving the consumer the choice of eating there or at home. Both provided food against ration cards, the latter being popular for the quality and variety of the food. More successful than the war kitchens were the 'people's kitchens' which provided a range of foods and somewhere to eat. In both countries much time was spent by social workers instructing women in the art of cooking without the basics – milk, eggs, fat.

Thoughts of food were uppermost in most people's minds, most of the time. By the end of the year there was a fodder shortage. Policemen could stop and search a parcel for provisions. Farmers would not sell produce because if they did not provide the army with their quota they lost their sugar allowance – essential to make jams to save fruit. Even the best Berlin restaurants were having trouble sourcing eggs, butter, tea and coffee, though they did manage to procure meat and fish. To make everyone feel better about the food shortage they were told it was ten times worse in Britain. And, when people noticed the amount of food being sent to British internees in Ruhleben Camp, they were told it was bluff to conceal the truth.

Like France, Germany was also feeling the cold. It too was short of fuel, but for different reasons. During 1916 it had exported large quantities to neutral countries and some to factories in the occupied zone to maintain production. As a result of poor planning, no stocks had been built up during the summer. Belatedly the government took action: non-war-work industries discontinued night work and overtime, shop-window lighting was virtually banned, hotel lights went out at midnight, unnecessary heating was banned and hot water was restricted to two hours a day. Shops and restaurants closed earlier, the lights went out at 9pm in apartment blocks and the streets were gloomy. Due to the difficulty in getting coal, many simply stayed in bed. Munich fared worse than Berlin: there all public buildings, cinemas and theatres were closed; there was no coal.

There was little snow clearing, few cars were to be seen, certainly no taxis as in Paris, just droshkies pulled by old and starving horses. The water pipes burst and, as in Paris, there were few plumbers. Fortunately for Berliners, unlike their counterparts in Munich, the theatres and art galleries were open, giving them a respite from the cold. One observer noted that 'the Art world did yeoman service to keep the people from going insane'. Theatrical productions in Berlin were many and varied, including Oscar Wilde and Shakespeare. Noticeably, there were no war plays.

In all three countries there were railway problems. Britain was short of locomotives and crews and coal, as was France. The situation was worst in Germany where the railway system was failing. With the onset of winter, coal demand from industrial areas and large towns caused congestion on the poorly maintained lines from the mines (experienced plate and track layers had been replaced by inexperienced PoWs and women). The deterioration in track servicing resulted in slower trains, the speed of which was reduced further by frost and snow. Insufficient coal got through, affecting the householder and the war effort. A knock-on effect was felt in towns that relied on electric trams: no coal, no electricity, difficulty in getting to work.

There was also a paper shortage and, in an attempt to save newsprint, newspaper posters were banned in March and the number of pages in newspapers reduced. This was coupled with a price rise for many of the leading papers. 'Waste paper became a marketable commodity. From Leeds it was reported that customers of whatever social standing were expected to bring their own bags or sheets of paper when shopping' – the reason being that waste paper by this time 'was nearly as valuable as the perfect product itself'. In Germany, where paper was equally short, officer PoWs made little bonfires of the Red Cross parcel boxes and newspapers they were sent, to annoy their guards.

War on such a scale required vast supplies of raw materials. Britain and France could import them but Germany relied on its own resources, plus those from captured territory and what it could buy from Norway and Sweden, a supply that would dry up later under British pressure. As a result, oil and metals were scarce. Providing light during the dark nights was difficult: the shortage of coal meant a corresponding shortage of electricity, there was little gas and even such a simple product as methylated spirit was scarce. The lack of oil affected the Catholic Church: sanctuary lamps in churches remained unlit. Such was the metal shortage that, across Germany, church bells and organ pipes were being removed for the war effort.

The continental warring powers also faced the threat of air raids. For the most part, British and French planes bombed industrial plants; naturally there were often civilian casualties. The Austrians bombed cities and military targets as did the Italians in retaliation. While the Germans did bomb targets in all the combat theatres in Europe, most of their efforts were against Britain.

By 1917 the Zeppelins had effectively been defeated, but they were now replaced by higher-flying airships, flying so high that in some cases they were inaudible and invisible. After the airships, came the Gotha aeroplanes and, later in the year, a handful of Riesen (giant) aircraft. Unlike the Zeppelins, the initial aeroplane raids were during the day, a time when people were up and about. How dangerous these early daylight raids could be is shown by the figures for the first Gotha raid on Britain and for the first raid on London. On 25 May, Gothas dropped a total of 139 bombs on Folkestone, killing 95 and injuring 290. In London, although Liverpool Street Station was the main objective, fatalities also occurred in other areas. One particularly tragic instance was the killing of 16 children and the wounding of 30 more when a bomb went through three floors of a school and exploded in the cellar where they were taking shelter. In total, 162 civilians were killed and 432 injured during this, the deadliest raid of the war.

After such initial German successes, air defences were strengthened and the Gothas later flew by moonlight. Although this impaired their accuracy, the raiders were still dangerous, especially in the East End where housing density was the highest and the homes offered less safety. The anticipation and the actuality of an air raid had two effects. Firstly, many moved to safer areas, like Brighton, during moonlit periods, and secondly, many families, taking their pets, moved into Underground stations for the night, often just in anticipation of a raid – something that was eventually banned by the government. Citizens of Dover hid from the enemy in the caves cut into the chalk cliffs.

Although the greater number of air raids was against targets in the south of England, no town was safe as navigation at night was difficult and mistakes were made. During the year, Hull, for example, experienced two raids which resulted in three (non-fatal) casualties. But for most of the country, there was little danger from aerial attack and the main cause for concern continued to be the blackout regulations.

Reading, like Brighton, was both far enough from London to escape from danger but close enough to return to if needed. Many chose not to return for the duration, putting unexpected demands on the local housing market. Their continued presence had an effect on schools and on the availability of food. Already suffering a housing shortage, the influx of people anxious to escape the air raids put a strain on Reading's ability to house them. Initially some slept in the station waiting room, others in the police station.

In many German towns there was the same housing pressure but not from air raids, although many industrial areas were bombed. Wartime movement of the population and lack of new homes caused a housing shortage that was further aggravated by the repatriation of German families previously living in Britain or the colonies. Such was the problem that, after a census of all available accommodation, compulsory billeting was introduced, much to the annoyance and inconvenience of both the resident and those billeted. Little account was taken of the billettees' suitability for the accommodation, thereby mixing classes, religions and regional affiliations.

As in 1916, there was considerable industrial unrest in Britain, especially about the subject of 'dilution' of skilled labour in engineering and munitions plants during the winter of 1916-17. Culminating in April and May, stoppages involved nearly 200,000 men and caused the loss of 1,500,000 working days. 'In some centres, military pickets were turned out to prevent troops on leave, notably Empire Servicemen, from attacking young strikers.' Not all the strikes were about money. At Messrs Burberry in Reading the dispute was about union recognition and most of the strikers were women.

To alleviate the problem, Lloyd George set up eight area commissions to investigate the causes of the discontent. A number of factors were highlighted: high food prices in relation to wages and the unequal distribution of food; the calling up of younger workers (who had thought themselves protected from the draft); the restriction on the mobility of labour; liquor restrictions; industrial fatigue due to weekly overtime and Sunday work; lack of adequate housing in some areas; lack of consideration for women workers by some employees; delays in granting pensions to soldiers; want of confidence in fulfilment of government pledges and the inadequacy of compensation under the Workmen's Compensation Act. Over the year there were 688 disputes involving 860,000 workers.

Thousands of miles away, the situation was similar in Australia. Although there were rumblings about German sympathisers causing problems with production, the main issues for workers were falling real wages and the perceived threat to pre-war working conditions. During the great strike of August 1917 the banners reflected these concerns: 'Preserve pre-war working conditions for the men at the front'; 'Don't be lashed with the speed-up whip'; 'The cost of living doesn't worry the speeders-up, does it?'; 'Australians will never be slaves'. The great strike began at a tram workshop in New South Wales and spread to several industries across several states. 'Over five weeks nearly 70,000 workers...had come out in sympathy' with tram men protesting against the introduction of a 'card system'. There were huge demonstrations in Sydney and Melbourne which later commentators believe shows that it was more about war-weariness, falling living standards, increasing costs, the conscription campaign and, because there were a lot of Irish settlers, the Dublin Uprising. After five weeks the strikers were forced to return to work, if they had not been fired or locked out.

Britain and Germany attempted to solve the manpower shortage in similar but different ways. In March 1917 the British Ministry of National Service started its work administering the National Service Scheme that was intended to introduce a system of National Industrial Service. This industrial army of volunteers was to be created to fill vacancies in industry caused by men being drafted. Launched with much publicity, it hoped for 500,000 volunteers but by mid-April only 163,000 had registered and, by August, only 20,000 of these had been placed in employment. Clearly the scheme was not a success. It was sharply criticised as a waste because of the excessive amount of administrative labour it employed to achieve so little.

The German version, Auxiliary Service, was a rigorously regimented law that was applied to men but encouraged women and children to become involved. This ignored the fact that tens of thousands, like their counterparts in Britain and France, were already replacing men in jobs in offices, industry, agriculture, driving trucks and labouring as navvies. Children were involved, notably in collecting salvage and scouring the countryside for edible wild foods. However, the scheme was successful and large numbers volunteered to work in factories, mines and steel works. The programme relied on even greater efforts by the civilian population, who were already deeply feeling the strain of the war.

In Germany 'after nearly two-and-a-half years virtually free of industrial disturbance, the country was suddenly hit by a wave of strikes.' The causes were mounting privations, war-weariness and working conditions.

'The first four months of the war saw strikes in the Ruhr, Berlin and elsewhere.' Mostly they were about food but some had political undertones. The Ruhr disturbances were so serious, troops were needed to restore order. Their demand was simple: more food or more money to buy black market food. In mid-April, the reduction in the bread ration resulted in a wave of strikes and non-violent demonstrations in Berlin and Leipzig. When promised an increase in the meat ration, most returned to work. In Leipzig the demonstrators also wanted the government to conclude a peace without annexation. They were offered a wage rise and fewer hours at work which they accepted. A strike in two Berlin weapons and munitions factories was less successful: they were ordered to return to work or face fines and imprisonment.

It was not always bad news. The launch of the submarine offensive was a morale boost and, a month later, the news of the Russian Revolution signified the end to the fighting on the Eastern Front. Hopes rose, but then America joined the war on the Allied side.

How did France compare? On the outbreak of war, France's factory laws and labour legislation had been suspended resulting in increasingly unpleasant working conditions. As in Britain and Germany, they had also suffered with rising prices and poor wages. In France availability of food was not really an issue – one diarist noted there were queues at the end of May to buy asparagus, strawberries and lamb – but prices certainly were. French workers were also affected by the Russian Revolution, the failure of the Nivelle offensive and anti-war agitators whose propaganda helped fuel the French soldiers' mutinies during May. Among the workers there was a similar 'surge of unrest, expressing itself in demonstrations, street parades, strikes and labour troubles'. While the army mutinies were about the slaughter, lack of leave, food and profiteers, the French workers, like their fellow workers in Britain, were concerned about working conditions, pay and the ever-increasing cost of living. By the end of June 1917, there had been 170 stoppages in factories in Paris and, for the whole year, 689 strikes compared to 98 in 1916: nearly 300,000 workers had been affected.

The comparison with Britain stops here. Although similarly taxed, in Britain there were no army mutineers or cloaked underworld helping men desert. Socialists reverted to pacifism and there was increasing Home Front criticism of the conduct of the war. Those troops lucky enough to get leave voiced their grievances, adding to the Home Front weariness and providing 'fertile ground for the pacifist-defeatist cliques' that were 'always looking for opportunities to plant their disruptive propaganda'. Although much of their effort was involved in getting anti-war material to the front, they were also active at the two main departure termini for the front, Gare de l'Est and Gare du Nord. As well as giving out anti-war literature they provided deserters with civilian clothing: 27,000 men deserted in 1917. They also dropped anti-war manifestos into civilian letter boxes in the Paris region. Most paid little heed to such blandishments even though many felt they could no longer believe the press, as a result of which, smaller, independent papers that did not follow the official line increased their circulation.

There were issues about France's war aims. How could the huge sacrifices be accepted without a clear end? While many pondered, there were defeatist groups actively undermining France's war effort: Marxists, internationalists, extreme left-wing factions, anarchists, pacifists, pro-Germans and enemy agents. In Britain, they were imprisoned or carefully monitored, but in France they had been left alone because their arrest might have caused problems during mobilisation.

The incident of a confiscated cheque from a German agent paymaster, returned by a government minister, brought the Ribot government down. 'The full extent of the internal dangers threatening France was to be revealed in the notorious "treason" trials that took place the following year.'

Women, known as midinettes, dressed in voluminous navy blue costumes and hats, parading along the Paris boulevards, were the first indicators of labour unrest. Each day the parade grew bigger. When they returned to work, other girls marched and picketed. While the demonstrations were mostly good-humoured, the marchers were quickly joined by revolutionary agitators as well as soldiers. For public protection, the police patrolled in force, directing crowd movement and protecting buildings. The government refused to arrest suspected troublemakers, believed to be helping foment unrest among the troops, because of a fear of revolution. However, while the government worried about the future of the war, those Parisians who could afford to enjoyed the high life at Versailles.

Like Germany, the demands of the arms factories reduced the availability of materials for other industries and the Home Front. The shortage of coal caused transport problems, and while peat, sawdust and wood met with limited success, there was more benefit from producing electricity from hydroelectric sources. France, like Britain and Germany, felt the manpower shortage acutely and also released men (over 300,000) from the front to help with agriculture and other industries – sugar factories, gasworks and potteries – anywhere they were needed to keep the nation going.

The cost of living in France was now 80 per cent higher than in pre-war times: less than in Britain and Germany, but even so many were struggling. In response coal distribution was controlled and coal tickets introduced. To help in a shortage, large quantities of firewood were stored in Paris. Bread rationing was introduced in towns of more than 20,000 and saccharin was now a common sugar substitute. Little of this affected the newly rich whose spending contrasted with the general wartime economy, especially in lavish clothing purchases – those with money affected a military look and even sweets 'were packed in boxes simulating shells, grenades and trench helmets'. In April 1918, a luxury tax would be imposed to attempt to curb such excesses.

Such were conditions in Germany that even the very rich 'had their troubles', leading colourless lives. Even charity work held little attraction and, even if money was raised, there was little to spend it on. Travel was difficult: the railways were in poor condition, fuel was scarce and a vast number of passes and certificates were needed. Everyone was treated equally.

France's losses were clearly seen on All Saint's Day. The solemn day of the dead 'was marked by long processions marching, in grey November weather, to lay wreaths on the tombs of dead soldiers. Black-clad mourners filled the churches and cemeteries.' Although one writer questioned whether it was wise to allow the country to plunge into a 'gulf of dark despair', the changing political scene brought forward a new leader, Clemenceau; a more capable leader than his predecessors. He liquidated defeatist cliques, silenced pessimists and set about renewing France's 'bruised and battered fighting spirit'.

In Britain, temporary memorials or shrines had appeared that commemorated the fallen. Britain's public schools had begun to think about permanent structures, Eton alone raising £100,000. Universities and employers were also recording the fallen, those serving, awards and commissions, which, at the end of the war, many would publish or commemorate in a permanent way. For example, by the end of the year, the Roll of Honour for Liverpool University stood at nearly 1,500, of whom 132 had died in service. It included four Victoria Crosses and one with a bar to the cross.

Whatever materialistic and manpower problems France and Britain had were eclipsed by those of the Central Powers who were 'living from hand to mouth' and where 'decay and rust had got the upper hand'. They were being strangled by the Allied blockade that forced them into 'ever more rigid self-sufficiency, without hope of renewal of supplies from outside'. However, this grip 'toughened the resolve of the stouter-hearted not to give in while the fighting men remained unbeaten'.

Although the role of women was the same in the major fighting powers, Britain led the way in assimilating them into the armed forces. As well as the many thousands of young women working in industry, there were many tens of thousands in uniform. On the civilian side were the policewomen, described as the 'true friends of the girls', whose successes in combating disorder, theft and drunkenness led to most cities in the country setting up their own female police service. In hospitals around Britain were the VADs of the Voluntary Aid Detachment, working as nurses or orderlies, many of whom came from middle- and upper-class backgrounds. And to assist with animal forage, hay baling, sack making, driving and tarpaulin sheet mending there was a Women's Forage Corps that had been formed in 1916. There were already women serving in the army at the start of the war – Queen Alexandra's Royal Army Nursing Corps, founded in 1897, as the Army Nursing Service.

Another pre-war corps that served in uniform and abroad was the First Aid Nursing Yeomanry; by 1918 there were 116 of them driving ambulances for the Red Cross. February saw the formation of the Women's Land Army, followed the next month by the formation of the biggest women's active service force, the Women's Army Auxiliary Corps (WAAC) from the embryonic 1914 Women's Legion of cooks and drivers. Later in the year the Admiralty set up the Women's Royal Naval Service (WRNS) under Katherine Furse. The women's services provided the armed forces with drivers, clerks, cooks, storekeepers, typists and many other roles, but the most important work was done by the WRNS who were involved in coding and decoding operations. There were also women serving in the Royal Flying Corps but it was not until April 1918 that they had their own service – the Women's Royal Air Force. Also in 1918 the WAAC became the Queen Mary's Army Auxiliary Corps, following their gallant behaviour during the German March offensive. This level of war participation was acknowledged in the Commons at the end of March. Approval was given for women's suffrage to be included in the electoral reforms at the end of the war.

While many women flocked to join the new military units, the majority stayed in munitions work. The dangers of working with high explosives have previously been mentioned. At Silvertown in January a multi-coloured fireball lit up the sky followed by a violent explosion, heard fifty miles away, and an earthquake tremor that reached the city. A square mile of buildings was razed to the ground; 2,000 people were made homeless, 69 killed and 450 injured, many of whom were women.

Even though women were releasing men for the front by joining the armed forces, the call-up was not producing sufficient men for the army. In order to make sure there were enough recruits, many of those previously classified as unfit for service were re-examined and given a classification that allowed them to serve at home, thereby releasing someone for the front. Later in the year, all doctors of military age were 'called up' to increase the number serving overseas. This was because of the danger of sending men home in hospital ships – increased U-boat activity resulted in the sinking of a number of hospital ships.

There were many unwilling to serve in the army. Some had genuine moral reasons, some political, some were self-preservationists; others had businesses to attend to. The tribunals were kept busy throughout the year assessing the validity of men's claims for deferral. Many were refused, some given leave to settle their affairs, and others were deferred for a number of months before they would be called up again. That left a small number of conscientious objectors who refused any form of work that would help the war.

Such was the feeling against them that farmers refused to have them on their land, or their labourers would not work with them. Many had spent long periods in prison for their beliefs. The answer was the establishment of camps for these unwanted men, of which the most publicised was on Dartmoor. 'Here in the spring 1917 a thousand men in overcoats, many of them newly out of gaol, were assigned to a land reclamation scheme on which they made indifferent progress. Their demands for ploughs instead of spades were not met.' Doing it by hand would take longer and keep them out of the way. Interestingly, one objector shot another, accidentally it appears, and at Knutsford a group of objectors armed with sticks, standing outside their centre, were rushed by a crowd and beaten with their own sticks.

During the year police powers were increased, giving them the power to arrest anyone or enter any premises at any time. Spies remained on everyone's mind and anyone could be accused. Married to a German, D.H. Lawrence was exiled from Cornwall, his house ransacked and his notebooks confiscated because he and his wife had been heard singing German songs – supposedly they were signalling to German submarines.

Entertainment was essential to keep up morale and, although sport helped take people's minds off things for a while, it was not to last. In May the Jockey Club suspended racing at the insistence of the War Cabinet and during the year the Oxford and Cambridge boat race, the Henley and Cowes Regattas, the football league cup final and county cricket all disappeared. In their place people could now see women playing organised football.

Like their divided views on conscription, narrowly rejected in late 1916, Australia was also divided about whether sport should continue. While it was understood that theatre and cinema were essential, the middle class could see no necessity to allow horse racing or prize fighting. As on British recruiting posters, the belief was that instead of playing sport, they should be fighting. However, unlike Britain, rowing survived, indeed the preliminary heats of the 1917 public schools' race attracted crowds of up to 50,000. Rugby league competitions continued throughout the year, while Union rugby did not. By the end of the year much football had also ceased. However professional football did continue in Western and Southern Australia.

As has been mentioned in previous volumes the flouting of convention increased during the war. For many the only compensation to the war was pleasure in whatever form it took. A new word was coined – 'flappers' – to describe the young girls who wore 'high heels, skirts up to their knees and blouses open to the diaphragm, painted, powdered, self-conscious, ogling'. There was a relaxation of sexual taboos caused by the now ephemeral state of life, the 'here today, gone tomorrow' attitude that was becoming more common, fuelled by broken homes, the new freedom of women, constant mobility, the crowding of men into camps and barracks, the loosening of social restraints and the strains and general tensions of wartime life. Life was cheap, so the moment was precious, and, as a result, by the end of the war the illegitimacy rate was 30 per cent above its pre-war baseline. The divorce rate rose rapidly but so too did the marriage rate. The Commissioner of Police in London stated that over the last three years, 19,000 women had been arrested on soliciting or similar charges and that they and the welfare societies were disturbed 'at the state of things in London's Parks and open spaces'.

Most indiscretions went unnoticed or warranted at most a brief paragraph in the local paper. However, in September was the sensational case of Lieutenant Malcolm, an officer of position and means. He had returned from France to deal with the alien scoundrel who was leading his wife astray, starting by horsewhipping him and challenging him to a duel. This did not deter Baumberg from trying to continue the liaison; neither did it stop Malcolm from settling the matter. Upon going to Baumberg's home, Malcolm shot him during a fracas. The Old Bailey jury found him not guilty of murder. He was not unique. Just two months later a soldier was acquitted for shooting his unfaithful wife. His rifle had accidentally discharged.

Juvenile delinquency had also increased, the rise being blamed on the absence of fathers and brothers to the war. However, the lack of such men was to some extent ameliorated by the work of groups such as the Scouts, the Boys' Brigade and other similar organisations.

Despite all this, there was less crime and certainly considerably less drunkenness, although cases did still feature in the papers like these from the *Berkshire Chronicle* and *Reading Standard*: George Smith, a nuisance, who was fined 10s for being drunk in a public place and Richard Hatton, found asleep in a doorway in a drunken condition, who was violent and used foul language. He was given the choice of seven days or 10s. More sensational was the case of Lily Applegate who, after being arrested on a string of alcohol-related charges, struggled with the police and made several attempts to kill herself by taking off most of her clothes and endeavouring to smother or strangle herself with them. Even when handcuffed with her hands behind her back for her own protection, she threw herself violently on the floor and placed her head in a vessel on the floor, causing her to need artificial respiration. When examined by a police doctor she was classed as very drunk. After pleading guilty she was fined 10s.

A change which was seen by some as unnecessary, and by others as a just reward, was the newly introduced Order of the British Empire. This was to be an award for non-military services, although there was later a military division that stopped soldiers being 'rewarded in the same list with swill contractors and canteen-keepers'. The publication of the first list was greeted in much the same way as recent honours lists: 'pleasure, irreverence and incredulity'. Again, mirroring modern events, the *New Statesman* noted that 'one had the impression that the general level of merit rose the lower one went in the grades' and that 'some of the new KBEs are laughing-stocks.' The *Herald,* a Socialist paper, noted the new reward was 'an order of chivalry from which it is the highest honour for a Labour man to be excluded'. How many thought of the Order is probably best summed up by a Scottish torpedo factory. When they were invited to select their own hero for the award, the unanimous choice was the lavatory attendant. Some even went as far as to turn it down. No doubt there was a similar feeling in Germany for those given awards.

Even with all the problems experienced on the Home Front and the general war-weariness, the prevalent attitude of the British people was that the struggle must go on. This was reflected in the attitude of the church and the government's rejection of German peace moves. The population had no time for pacifists, or for British peace moves as made by Lord Lansdowne in November, or International Socialism, as the Seamen's Union demonstrated when it refused to man the ship taking Ramsay MacDonald to the International Socialist conference in Stockholm. In fact resolution was stiffened by the arrival of American troops in the middle of August. However, the statement by an Australian historian that 'by the end of 1917 Australians seemed emotionally exhausted', was probably true of the vast majority of the people in the world on both sides and in neutral countries. It had affected most people in some way.

Then, once again it was Christmas, the fourth of the war. With the shortages, would people be able to or feel able to celebrate a season of goodwill to all men? It was unlikely given the sacrifices made during the year. Writing from France in his column in the *Hull Times,* Major Fairfax-Blakeborough summed up the season of goodwill in which hatred reigned supreme: 'the angels weep and the devils laugh.'

For many it was more a time of despondency. Though Caroline Playne recorded at the time that there was a spirit of 'grin-and-bear-it' abroad, she noted in agreement that like Australians, in Britain 'most folk looked worn-out and sorrowful'.

In an attempt to make Christmas a little better than the previous one, the Ministry of Food planned a set Christmas dinner of French rice soup, filleted haddock, roast fowl and vegetables, plum pudding and caramel custard at 10 shillings for four people. But even this could not stop Christmas 1917 being the gloomiest of the war. While in Paris, there was 'as much gloom as hope' and 'in many parishes…there was no midnight mass. The streets were badly lighted, the churches cold, and there was constant fear of the Zeppelins.'

With the signing of the Russian armistice in December, many Germans hoped for peace. However, Princess Blücher noted that 'Christmas was…but a sorry season'. Even with the armistice and the peace message of Christmas, there was no let up from the suffering. While British and French civilians were experiencing the worst Christmas of the war, it was far worse for those on the Home Front in Germany, as one writer explained: 'One of the most terrible of our many sufferings was having to sit in the dark…It became dark at four in the winter. It was not light until eight o'clock. Even the children could not sleep all that time. One had to amuse them as best one could, fretful and pining as they were from under-feeding. And when they had gone to bed we were left shivering with the chill which comes from semi-starvation and which no additional clothing seems to alleviate.'

As in the other three war Christmases, everything that was possible was done at war hospitals across the country 'to make it bright and cheerful' for the wounded. Possibly they were more cheerful as they were, at least for the present, safe. For those able, there was a Christmas meal, games and other entertainment provided for free, and in some cases gifts from Santa himself.

As 1917 passed into history, many must have pondered on what had happened, but most would be looking to the future, hoping that the war would finally be over by Christmas, not knowing that the army, even with the Americans arriving in ever increasing numbers, expected to continue fighting well beyond that. The year had seen shortages and an almost constant increase in the cost of living; most were feeling the pinch, even those in well-paid munitions jobs. Probably the only thing they were all certain about was that it would not get easier; it would be more expensive to live and there would be more casualties and sorrow. In the Central Powers, food shortages and the spread of normally treatable diseases would increase the civilian death rate. This would not be unique to them; the world would shortly feel the effects of an influenza pandemic that would kill more people across the world than all the fighting did. In order to source sufficient metal, door locks and latches were taken for melting down. The winter weather would get worse and those countries not yet rationing would be forced to do so. In Britain the Retail Food Price (RFP – a monthly index of price increases on staple foods since the start of the war) stood at 106 per cent, a rise of 10 percentage points over the year.

It may not have looked rosy but neither side was ready to admit to anything other than total victory. The Reverend Canon Fowler of Earley St. Peter's Church summed up the year for his parishioners: 'How the war drags on from week to week, month to month, and how, in spite of all, it finds us determined as ever not to give in until an end has been made to the menace of tyranny and despotism.' Unlike previous years when the editorials for the coming year were about victory, neither the Reading nor the Hull papers, 200 miles north, said anything of the sort. The *Hull Daily Mail* for 31 December 1917 merely featured a short poem:

Ring out false pride in place and blood,
The civic slander, and the spite;
Ring in the love of truth and right,
Ring in the common love of good.

Canon Fowler's words that 'the war dragged on' were no doubt reinforced across the country by countless local papers.

1917 had been born with great expectation and hope, 1918 was met with resignation and acceptance of further privation and a continuation of the struggle. In France, Clemenceau summed up the year from the Allied perspective: 'We are still in profound darkness…The year started in mist. It is ending in fog. No matter. Let us go on hoping all the same.' There was no light in the tunnel yet. All the warring nations 'looked to a coming year in which victory seemed as remote as ever.'

Section 1
Recruiting and departure

GWI-HF_4 Wives and sweethearts of the 'combed-out' men accompanying the recruits. An image reminiscent of the previous January. Some of these men would have volunteered under the Derby Scheme in late 1915 and were only now being called up.

GWI-HF_5 The original caption was 'splendid recruits for the British Army: Policemen who have just joined the London Scottish'. These were officers who had just been released for military service. They were a splendid group of men that compared very favourably with recent drafts to the German Army.

GWI-HF_8 With America entering the war, British subjects were able to enlist at the British recruiting office in New York. As there were reciprocal agreements about foreign citizens being called up, many volunteered.

GWI-HF_6 Among the first drafts of the year was Jimmy Wilde, the famous boxer, and holder of the Fly Weight Championship. He had been graded as only suitable for garrison duty abroad but had been upgraded to category A upon request (he went on to serve as an instructor at Sandhurst, dying aged 76 in 1969).

GWI-HF_10 A previously untapped pool of recruits: women. Here new volunteers to the Women's Army Auxiliary Corps are being kitted out. Known as WAACs or Brownies, because of their uniform, they took over rear-echelon tasks that would release a man for the front.

WI-HF_7 Enlistment in French overseas territory was voluntary, so great efforts were made to attract recruits.

WI-HF_9 A scene reminiscent of the rush to volunteer in Britain before the introduction of conscription. Volunteers enlisting at Toronto in September 1917, before the Canadian Military Service Act came into force.

WI-HF_11 In the early summer of 1917, a Women's Army Auxiliary Corps was raised officially to serve with the field army in various capacities, chiefly in connection with clerical and telegraphic work, but also for other branches such as carpentry and motor-driving. These photographs show new recruits and a company ready for France.

GWI-HF_13 Mirroring British citizens enlisting in New York, here Americans of military age are registering for service at the Connaught Rooms in Great Queen Street.

GWI-HF_12 Britain in 1917 was an armed camp. These are the young sailors at Shotley Naval Training establishment in August 1917. In the centre is the Bishop of London and Rear-Admiral Cayley CB, who w paying the boys a visit.

GWI-HF_15 Two of the earliest recruits after the American declaration of war are seen carrying their kit.

JOIN NOW · RECRUIT TO WAR STRENGTH · NO EXPENSE · WALK IN

GWI-HF_17 Early recruits for the American Army leaving a New York recruiting office. There was not the rush to join the army on the declaration of war that there had been in Britain.

GWI-HF_19 A pair of 'before and after' photographs: new recruits at Newport Naval Training Station.

GWI-HF_20 The same recruits ten days later.

GWI-HF_16 Chicago's first draft of recruits marching down Michigan Avenue.

GWI-HF_24 A display of Canadian regimental colours on Wolfe's monument in Westminster Abbey, left by the departing battalions.

GWI-HF_18 Across America, as in Britain, new camps sprang up to house the new soldiers.

GWI-HF_23 The Duke of Connaught, Governor-General of Canada from 1911 to 1916, is watching a march past of the Canadian Scottish during their stay at an English training camp.

GWI-HF_25 A Royal Party watching an attack display behind a shell barrage.

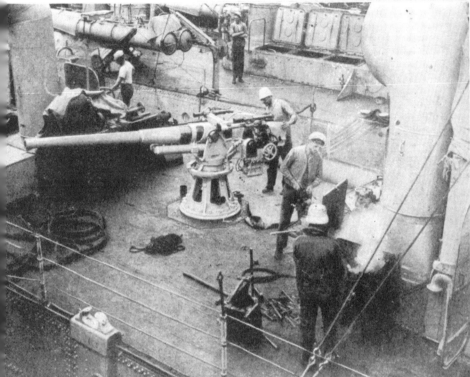

GWI-HF_22 American destroyers in an English port getting ready to go to sea. Within a month of the United States entering the war, American ships were assisting in the campaign against the U-boats.

GWI-HF_21 New recruits to Britain were the Portuguese Army. Here they have just detrained and are marching to camp.

Section 2
Home Defence

GWI-HF_28 Cleaning and polishing rifles and bayonets in the New York Armoury, for America's army.

GWI-HF_26 General Pershing (centre) inspecting the Guard of Honour furnished by the Welsh Fusiliers on his arrival at Liverpool as commander-in-chief of the American Expeditionary Force.

GWI-HF_27 Many older men volunteered to serve in the volunteer battalions raised by line regiments. The ranks also included many who were not fit for the army or were in reserved occupations. These men are in the volunteer London Scottish.

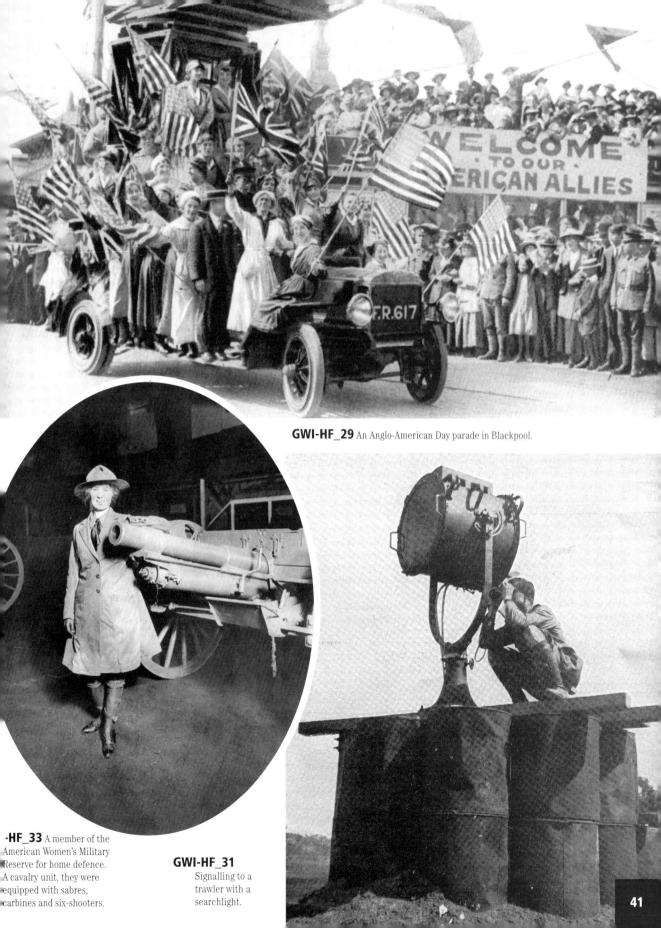

GWI-HF_29 An Anglo-American Day parade in Blackpool.

·HF_33 A member of the American Women's Military Reserve for home defence. A cavalry unit, they were equipped with sabres, carbines and six-shooters.

GWI-HF_31 Signalling to a trawler with a searchlight.

GWI-HF_32 Precautions against German air-raids: an RNAS unit patrolling the coast in an airship, and two anti-aircraft guns.

GWI-HF_35 A similar scene in Italy. These anti-aircraft guns were used to defend Venice against Austrian attacks.

GWI-HF_34 An anti-aircraft battery manned by both naval and military men.

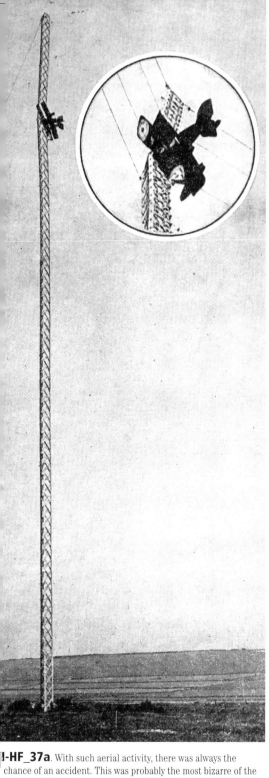

GWI-HF_30 American citizens enrolling as special police in the armoury of the 69th New York Regiment. Their first job was to relieve the National Guard who where stationed at the Catskill Aqueduct.

GWI-HF_37 The faces of those who tackled the German air threat appeared in the papers. These airmen were decorated for their part in the destruction of the super-Zeppelin, L48, on 17 June 1917. Above is Second Lieutenant Holder, who received the MC for his part in the destruction of the airship. Sergeant Ashby, below, received the MM.

I-HF_37a. With such aerial activity, there was always the chance of an accident. This was probably the most bizarre of the war: On 14 September, a seaplane collided with a Poulsen mast and remained wedged in it. The pilot, acting-Flight-Commander E.A. de Ville, was rendered unconscious and thrown out onto one of the wings. Seaman Rath, assisted by Seaman Knoulton and Seaman Abbott, climbed up 100 feet, then the two latter hoisted him in a boatswain's chair over 300 feet. Seaman Rath climbed out and held the pilot until the other two arrived and passed him a gantline. With this he secured the pilot and lowered him to the ground. Rath was awarded the Albert Medal in gold for saving the airman: Knoulton and Abbott received the Albert Medal.

GWI-HF_36 This army anti-aircraft detachment claimed to have shot down a Zeppelin. Between 4 August 1914 and 24 October 1917, the government stated that the British defences had destroyed sixteen Zeppelins.

GWI-HF_38 Raven House, Adderley, after being used as an auxiliary hospital, was given to the Cavell Committee as a rest home for nurses.

Section 3
Raids and U-boats

GWI-HF_40 A magazine holding six rockets.

GWI-HF_41 A model 'dug-out' built near the YMCA in the Strand. It was advertising 'Hut Day', a collection to buy huts for the troops abroad.

GWI-HF_42 Twenty feet below the surface, in chalk pits, the inhabitants of Ramsgate were able to sleep in absolute safety from the bombs.

GWI-HF_39 At 8.30 am on Sunday, 22 July, as part of a trial early warning system, 237 one-pound sound-bombs were fired 300 feet into the air fr 79 London Fire Brigade stations. 'Take cover' notices were also shown the police at the same time. At 9.45 am the 'All Clear' was displayed. T fireman is about to fire a sound-bomb.

GWI-HF_43 An air raid drill: schoolgirls practising carrying a wounded schoolfellow.

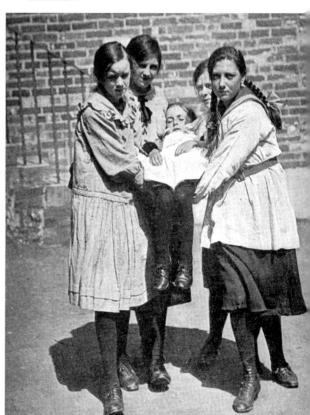

GWI-HF_44 An air raid practice at a London institution.

GWI-HF_45 Miss Margaret McMillan CBE leading a train of small children to a dug-out, or smuggler's cave.

GWI-HF_49 Jules Boiteux was out shooting when the Zeppelin L49 descended near him. He realised the captain was attempting to destroy the craft and, holding a loaded shotgun, shouted 'Stop, or I fire!' The commander threw down his gun, held up his arms and shouted 'Kamerad!, Kamerad!'.

GWI-HF_50 The commander of one of the two aeroplanes brought down during the early morning Gotha raid on 6 December 1917.

GWI-HF_47 The Austrians attacked targets in Italy and caused severe damage to many historic buildings. Sandbags were the usual method of defence for a building. Here they are protecting the tomb of the Doge Giovanni Mocenigo, in Sante Giovanni e Paolo, in Venice.

GWI-HF_48 The lights of London seen from Hendon.

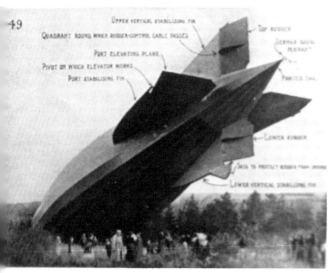

GWI-HF_53 A view of the Zeppelin L49 after it was shot down.

GWI-HF_46 A raid rehearsal: marching to shelter.

GWI-HF_53a Training fitters for the RFC in Reading.

GWI-HF_52 A view of a Zeppelin brought down in France.

GWI-HF_51 The remains of one of the Gothas that was shot down on 6 December 1917.

GWI-HF_59 A view of the damage caused to a house during a raid on London: a house in Hither Green after the raid of 19-20 October 1917.

GWI-HF_55 The Mayor of London, with General Sir Francis Lloyd, heading the funeral procession for the victims of a Zeppelin raid.

GWI-HF_60 Scouts on bicycles cycled around cities, sounding the 'All Clear'.

GWI-HF_61 A car driven by a special constable is being used to let the public know it is safe to leave shelters.

GWI-HF_62 Cars were also used to give the public notice of an impending raid.

GWI-HF_54 A poor-quality photograph of the largest Gotha raid on London on 7 July 1917. The raid caused considerable anger about the lack of defences and the lack of proper warnings. The planes formed up over Epping Forest and bombed the East End and City of London, killing 54 people. It prompted an anti-German riot.

GWI-HF_65 Possibly the last photo of the sailing ship *Cooroy* before it sank: research indicates there was no loss of life.

GWI-HF_56 Transporting air raid victims to hospital after the raid of 7 July.

GWI-HF_64 A captured U-boat crew being escorted to a PoW camp.

GWI-HF_63 A stranded U-boat was set on fire and partly blown up during August 1917 on the beach near Calais. The crew were taken prisoner.

GWI-HF_71 Survivors from HMAT *Ballarat* pose at an army training camp.

GWI-HF_69

Survivors from the SS *California* sunk on 7 February 1917 by U-boat *U-85*. The three children lost their mother and eldest sister; thirty-nine other passengers and crew lost their lives.

GWI-HF_70 Australian troops waiting to get into the lifeboats on HMAT *Ballarat* as the boat was sinking after a U-boat attack.

GWI-HF_68 Some of the rescued crew and staff of the hospital ship *Rewa*.

Section 4
Propaganda

GWI-HF_73 A propaganda photograph of a captured U-boat. It was cut into sections for ease of transport and was used to help advertise 'Liberty Bonds'.

GWI-HF_72 In order to stimulate American public interest, shortly after the declaration of war, a British exhibition of war-trophies toured major American cities. This photo was taken in Atlantic City. Among the exhibits were a German sea-mine and torpedo, a gun taken from the Emden, a trench howitzer, the floats of a wrecked British seaplane, and numerous relics and trophies: war-worn helmets, uniforms, rifles, and other equipment, plus photographs and parts of the first Zeppelin brought down in England.

GWI-HF_74 A British tank was taken to America and driven around New York to stimulate investment in 'Liberty Bonds'.

GWI-HF_75 A Home Front propaganda postcard about how everyone was pulling together.

GWI-HF_76 A tank was also shipped to Canada to help bolster the war effort. Here it is used to show the power of the Allies and what they would do to the Germans.

GWI-HF_77 The display of captured war materiel was always a good way to boost morale. Here a captured German aircraft is pulled through the streets of London as part of the annual Lord Mayor's Parade.

GWI-HF_80 There was great propaganda to be had on the arrival of American troops in Britain. Here the American flag is flying on Plymouth Hoe on 4 August 1917, the third anniversary of the war.

GWI-HF_78 Another exhibit for the Lord Mayor's parade was a 250m trench mortar captured in September.

GWI-HF_81 The arrival of a United States medical unit for the Western Front: nurses driving to their hotel in London.

GWI-HF_82 On 15 August, the newly arrived American soldiers marched through London to a hearty welcome from the assembled crowds. Most of them came from the mid-west and it was noted that they were all volunteers and mostly clean-shaven.

GWI-HF_83 On 19 April, on the occasion of the Anglo-America service at St. Paul's Cathedral, the Union Jack and the Stars and Stripes flew together over the Houses of Parliament. Speaking in 1887, John Bright declared that an alliance between America and Great Britain would be one of the greatest factors for peace the world had ever known.

GWI-HF_84 King George took the salute as the American troops marched past Buckingham Palace on 15 August.

GWI-HF_85 On their arrival in Paris the American troops were greeted with the same enthusiasm as they had been in London.

Section 5
Refugees and Occupation

GWI-HF_86 Madame Pellequer, a school teacher of the Maucourt neighbourhood, is seen here being decorated with the Croix de Guerre before the local Territorials and her own schoolchildren. She assumed civil charge of the village during the German occupation, acted as mayor, and bravely prevented German excesses by her force of character.

GWI-HF_87 One of several timber houses built by French troops after the German retreat from Maucourt.

GWI-HF_88 As the Allies advanced through the newly liberated villages, during the German retreat, the villagers gathered their belongings and moved back to safer villages, returning when the battle had moved on.

GWI-HF_89 Later in the year, during the Battle of Cambrai, the same happened. Here villagers are leaving the Cambrai battle area during the fighting.

GWI-HF_90 The fighting in Macedonia also created refugees. Here they are quartered in the nave of a church in Agia Pareskevi.

GWI-HF_91 Life in the occupied zone was frugal and controlled. Many of the shops were taken over by the Germans for their own men. This is Maison Ducrot, previously a carpet and bedding shop, and in 1917 a shop for German officers.

GWI-HF_93 Belgian women and children employed in a mill at Moustier under German military control. The picture is open to interpretation but the original caption writer was certain that it poignantly suggested 'the terrorism under which the people lived – the girls apprehensively awaiting the result of a colloquy between one woman and a soldier, which an officer is grimly watching.'

GWI-HF_92 A scene in a food centre in Belgium organised by the American Relief Commission. The old men were able, at this centre, to remain and eat their allowance of food, instead of having to carry it away for consuming at home.

GWI-HF_94 A store taken over by Lines of Communication troops in St. Quentin became a war market selling, every Friday, live carp, fresh sea fish, quality oysters, fresh vegetables, Brussels grapes, southern fruits.

Section 6
Casualty and Captivity

GWI-HF_95 Munitions casualties were not only caused by large explosions, there were many deaths from accidents. Here fellow munitionettes pay their respects at the funeral of a fellow worker.

GWI-HF_96 The funeral at Manor Park of a member of the WAAC, Miss Dorothy Reed.

GWI-HF_97 An air raid victim being helped by his mother.

GWI-HF_98 After an air raid: running to get the child to a doctor.

GWI-HF_100 Relativ
of some of the
children killed in th
Zeppelin raid.

GWI-HF_99 At midday on 13 June 1917, fourteen Gothas, during the first daylight fixed-wing air raid, dropped bombs over the East End of London, killing 104 people, seriously injuring 154, and slightly injuring a further 269. A bomb hit a school in Poplar, killing 18 children, 16 aged between four and six. Their funeral procession is turning into the street where they had been killed.

GWI-HF_101 Over 500 wreaths were sent from all parts of the country to the funerals of the schoolchildren killed. The Bishop of London read a message from the King and Queen and demanded 'the strongest punishment for the perpetrators and designers of these raids, who were the murderers of the children'. While sailors carried the coffins to the grave, two RFC aircraft flew over.

GWI-HF_102 The fune
procession for some o
the 98 men killed on
September, when a bc
was dropped on their
barracks in the Sheer
Chatham area.

GWI-HF_104 By 1917 the transfer of the wounded on the Home Front
was a well-organised process. When a train of wounded was due, the
ambulances were there to take them to their destination.

GWI-HF_103 Naval bombardments and long-range shelling also caused casualt
This French woman was wounded during an artillery bombardment and is bei
taken to the local hospital.

GWI-HF_105 Th
wounded were
still looked afte
by voluntary
organisations. F
are two motorcy
ambulances
belonging to the
Nottingham Cor
of the St. John's
Ambulance Brig

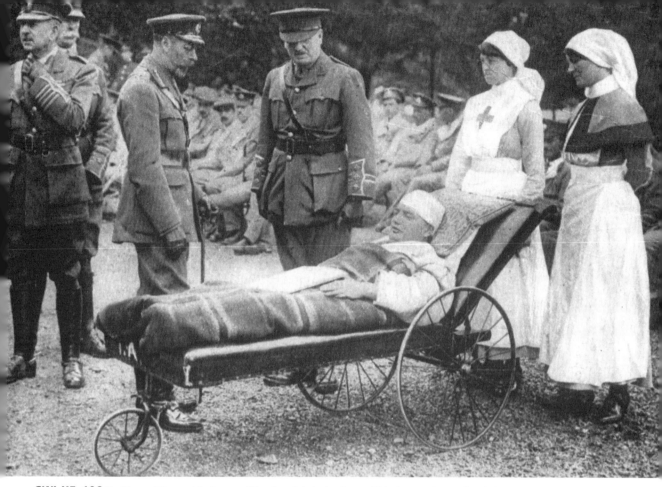

GWI-HF_106 The King and Queen visited many military hospitals during the war. This photograph was taken during a visit to Netley.

GWI-HF_107 The women of the higher echelons of society helped the war effort in many ways; some even took to nursing rather than fund-raising. This is the Marchioness of Ormonde who worked in her hospital for soldiers with facial injuries, in Upper Brook Street, London.

GWI-HF_108 The original caption for this picture was 'Royal consideration for the wounded'. Most of the men obviously have leg wounds (they are using crutches) and are expected to stand, in the rain, while the Queen walks by with an umbrella – Royal consideration indeed!

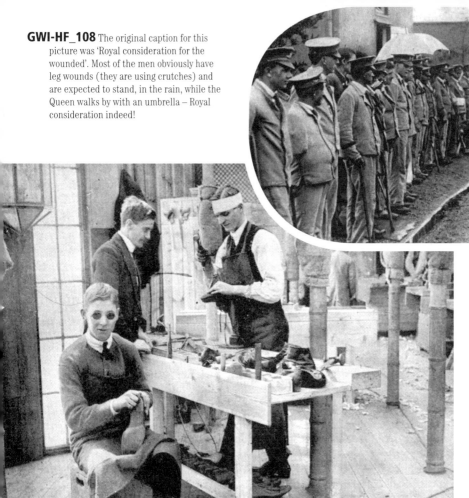

GWI-HF_109 Men who had become blind in the war were retrained at St. Dunstan in Regent's Park. These men are learning boot-repairing, one of the many occupations taught to minimise their dependence on others.

GWI-HF_110 A similar scene in Canada, invalided soldiers being taught a trade. This was a chauffeur-training class at Montreal Technical High School.

GWI-HF_111 These two discharged soldiers are lifting and carting potatoes on the land of Cheshire County College of Agriculture. The college provided a general training course in agriculture for discharged personnel.

GWI-HF_112 Pictured at the Eccentric Club Hostel in Hackney, these 'maimed soldiers' are engaged in making ladies' handbags and fancy articles.

GWI-HF_113 Although neutral, Holland was pro-British. Westgate House in Beckenham was bought by Dutch citizens living in Britain, for the use of convalescent British officers.

GWI-HF_114 One of the rooms in Westgate House.

GWI-HF_117 There were many ways to stop wounded soldiers becoming bored. Here convalescents are joyriding in the snow near London.

GWI-HF_116 Wounded soldiers needed entertaining. Here discharged sailors, who fought in the Jutland battle, were describing their experiences during a concert at a Birmingham War Hospital garden party.

GWI-HF_115 A scene at North End, Hampstead, home of Lord Leverhulme. This pastoral scene was part of a fête to raise funds for the Hampstead and North West London General Hospital. Naturally there was a large attendance.

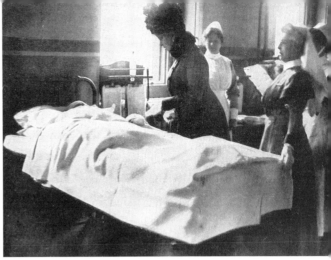

GWI-HF_121 During the visit to Manchester, the King and Queen visited the Manchester Royal Infirmary. She is seen here talking to a seriously wounded soldier.

GWI-HF_118 During the better weather, there was always the local fête for passing a few hours. At Sidcup sports, a one-legged soldier supports himself while pelting an effigy of the Kaiser with small rocks.

GWI-HF_122 Throughout the war, PoWs were either exchanged or transferred to either Holland or Switzerland where they were interned and not held as prisoners, although they could not leave. These are new arrivals at Château D'Oex, Switzerland. From right to left: Sohar Singh (Punjabis), Sergeant Cox (Lincolnshire Regiment), Dalbahadar Thapa (Gurkhas), Harkuman Libu (Gurkhas), Ahmet Khan (Punjabis), Sadak Khan (Sikhs) and Margulat Khan (Punjabis).

GWI-HF_120 It was not possible to decorate every soldier at Buckingham Palace or in Hyde Park so the King and Queen often combined their visits to cities and hospitals with award ceremonies. This presentation took place in Manchester during a visit.

GWI-HF_123 Clearly showing their pro-Allies stance, these Belgian soldiers interned in Holland are keeping their arms clean during their storage.

GWI-HF_124 Interned French soldiers employed in agricultural work at Brienz, Switzerland.

GWI-HF_126 In order to counter the shortage of labour in Britain, German PoWs were employed in a range of occupations not directly related to the war effort.

GWI-HF_127 With the declaration of war German sailors interned in America became prisoners overnight. Here they are setting out from Fort McPherson, Georgia, on their day's tasks under armed guard. Thei first task was to build their own accommodation.

GWI-HF_125 German sailors saved from the sea by men of HMS *Broke* and HMS *Swift*, after a Channel battle.

GWI-HF_128 German PoWs in Britain also built their own huts before being employed. Here they are at work on a farm in Hainault Forest, Essex.

GWI-HF_130 British PoWs received regular parcels from home which provided them with essential food and clothing. If they had had to rely solely on their captors, many more would have died in captivity. This scene is in Peel House in Hull, where relatives could arrange for a parcel to be sent to a PoW.

GWI-HF_129 This cheerful group of German PoWs is involved in hedging and ditching. Such men were paid in accordance with the Hague Convention and received extra rations for manual labour. No wonder they look happy.

GWI-HF_131 Photographs of PoWs in the newspapers were popular. Often the members of the group were identified and a letter included. The photos always showed the prisoners in the best light, well-fed and clothed, often in stark contrast to the reality. The original caption read: 'a gratifying feature of this picture is that these prisoners look well cared for.' After the war, the truth would come out.

GWI-HF_134 One of the offices in the interior of the Agence des Prisonnie de Guerre, in Geneva.

GWI-HF_132 Photographs such as this were important reminders to the people on the Home Front and also a useful way of knowing what had happened to someone. The man with the bandaged arm is Corporal E. Bryant, 2nd Queen's Regiment, of 2, Whittington Cottages, Lower Village Road, South Ascot. His parents received two conflicting reports: Killed in action on 14 July 1916, and three weeks later that he was a PoW. The arrival of the picture confirmed the latter report was true.

GWI-HF_133 In order to keep a track of the various PoWs the Red Cross opened up a PoW agency staffed by volunteers. The picture shows how many were involved in the work during 1917.

GWI-HF_135 Those who refused to enlist were incarcerated in prisons. This group of conscientious objectors were trenching and clearing ground on Dartmoor. They were quartered in Princetown prison. As a result of the 'latitude in the employment of their time' there was much hostile criticism and public protest meetings at Plymouth.

GWI-HF_136 This is the funeral of one of the British sailors killed in the battle, which included close-quarters fighting when *Broke* rammed *G42* and the two jammed together before the torpedo boat sank.

In Memoriam.

WILLIAM HENRY JACKSON

(Queen's Westminster Rifles).

WHO FELL IN ACTION, MARCH 20th, 1917.

"Greater love hath no man than this, that a man lay down his life for his friends.

r. & Mrs. JACKSON,
99 Forburg Road,
Clapton Common, N.16.

GWI-HF_138 For those who could afford them, cards were made in memory of the fallen throughout the war. This is Private Richard John Brown of the Royal Welsh Fusiliers, who died in France on 27 September 1917, aged 20. He was the youngest son of Mr and Mrs E. Brown, 2, Commercial Road, Cadoxton.

GWI-HF_139 A large 'In Memoriam' card produced by Private Jackson's parents.

GWI-HF_137 The funeral of British sailors who lost their lives in the 2nd Battle of Dover Strait took place at Dover on 24 April. Readers of the magazine it was originally printed in were informed unofficially that 22 British and 28 Germans had died and that 10 officers and 108 men were made prisoner.

GWI-HF_140 German 'In Memoriam' cards tended to have a set pattern of either a double-sided sheet or a fold-out card: most included a photograph of the deceased. Michael Stegbauer died as a result of a head wound on 30 November 1917, aged 19. The picture clearly shows that he had joined the army before his age group was called, probably when he was 17.

Zur frommen Erinnerung
im Gebete an den
ehr- und tugendsamen Jüngling
Michael Stegbauer,
Soldat in einem bayer. Inf.-Rgt.,
Gütlerssohn von Rinkam,
welcher am 30. November 1917 infolge Kopfschuß in Flandern im Blütenalter von 19 Jahren den Heldentod fürs Vaterland starb.
R. I. P.
Kühn zogst Du aus zum schweren Streit
Fürs Vaterland völl Treue.
Wir hofften auf ein Wiedersehn
Mit jedem Tag aufs neue.
Doch ach, nun kommst Du nimmermehr!
Dein hoffnungsfrohes Leben
Du musstest es dem Vaterland
Wie viele andre geben.
Wir weinen leis und hoffen still
Daß über jenen Sternen
Wir sieggekrönt Dich wiedersehn
Dort in des Himmels Fernen.

✠

Gedenket im Gebete

des Herrn

Franz Scheuchenpflug

Bauerssohn in Unterniederndorf,
Pfarre St. Leonhard, O.-Oe.
beim k. k. Schützenregiment Linz Nr. 2

welcher am 21. Juli 1917 im Kampfe
gegen Italien bei Mohorini (Istrien),
23 Jahre alt, sein junges Leben für Gott,
Kaiser und Vaterland hingegeben hat.

Gar weit von meiner Heimat mußt' ich sterben,
Des Feindes Kugel brachte mir den Tod.
Ich fiel inmitten meiner Kameraden
Und zog mit diesen heim zum lieben Gott.

Die Sternlein weihn mir ihren heil'gen Schimmer
Und grüßen meines Grabes stillen Ort.
O, seid getrost, es leuchtet mir für immer
Das ew'ge Licht in meiner Heimat dort

So lebt nun wohl, lieb' Eltern und Geschwister
Und Trost sei euch in eurem tiefen Weh!
Nur eine kleine Weile wird es dauern,
Bis daß ich froh euch alle wiederseh' !

Akad. Preßvereinsdruckerei Linz. 5614 17

VI-HF_143 A special burial ground, next to the Woking Mosque, was provided for Muslim troops who died of their wounds in Britain.

MAJOR BASIL ZIANI DE FERRANTI, M.C.,
R.G.A. Son of Dr. S. Z. de Ferranti, The Hall, Baslow, Derbyshire.

CAPT. MAURICE LAKE HILDER, M.C., Royal Fusiliers. Son of Mr. and Mrs. Edward Hilder, Wellington Road, Regent's Park.

GWI-HF_142 Local papers and national magazines often carried pictures of those reported dead.

Section 7
Women at War

GWI-HF_144 Three munitionettes pose in their work coats, displaying their 'On War Service' badges.

GWI-HF_147 Although opposed by many workmen, women quickly replaced men in many skilled jobs. Here a woman is screwing the breech screw for a 60-pounder howitzer.

GWI-HF_148 Miss Lily Smith and Miss Annie Rose, shown here being 'chaired' by fellow workers, were awarded the OBE for their work. The original caption commented that they had both 'well earned their honours. Miss Smith had lost her left hand; and Miss Rose two of her fingers.'

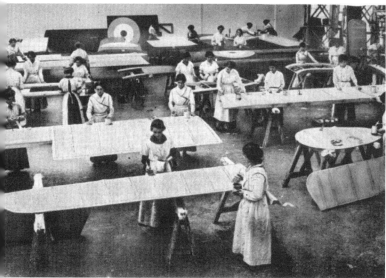

GWI-HF_145 The King was a popular figure during the war because he met the 'common people'. Here he is about to inspect the firefighting unit of a big factory. Of the six in the photograph, those without a hard helmet are women: the men are wearing metal helmets for protection, to show rank, possibly because the women were not their equals and could not actually fight any fire that broke out?

GWI-HF_146 An important job, that had to be painstakingly done, was doping the fabric to make it tight and waterproof. The fumes from the dope were strong, flammable and poisonous: the work was mostly carried out by women in unventilated workshops.

GWI-HF_150 The war broke down many barriers. How many women would have played football before the war? Here the munitionettes of the fuse-making department of a munitions factory are playing the ladies from another department, the 'Mechanicals.'

-HF_149 As most of those employed in munitions factories were female, it made sense to have a women's police force in the larger factories. Pictured are such a group.

GWI-HF_151 Hard winter work: digging potatoes out of the clamp with a special tool and then sorting, grading and checking for disease – riddling potatoes.

GWI-HF_152 Few jobs on the farm were not taken over by women: feedin[g] the pigs.

GWI-HF_153 A hard, back-breaking job, in the cold: spreading manure on the fields.

GWI-HF_154 After a few minutes' instruction on the tractor, Mrs Douglas was able to drive and her husband guide the plough on their farm near Reigate. The special wartime tractor could plough five acres a day, haul a five-ton load, and in a harvest field cut up t[o] twenty-five acres daily.

GWI-HF_155 Most ploughing was done by hand. In this picture Miss D. Truscott, of St. Veep, Cornwall, is operating a two-horse plough. She was a local celebrity. At just 14, one of the youngest members of the Women's Land Army, she had already 'won three first prizes at agricultural demonstrations in Cornwall – for harnessing and driving two horses in a wagon; for harrowing; and for the prize costume, of showerproof washable twill, which she is wearing.' In 1916 she had raked eighty acres of corn without help.

GWI-HF_156 A member of the Women's Land Army is haymaking with a horse-rake on a farm in Suffolk.

GWI-HF_157 The record plum crop of 1917 was saved by the government installing a pulping plant at Maidstone which had a capacity of sixty tons a day. The picture shows the factory workers unloading an early-morning load.

GWI-HF_158 Lord French had a reputation as a womaniser and the original caption may have been alluding to this. Here he is shown at a motor-transport parade of women drivers. 'Lord French has from the first shown keen interest in and appreciation of the war-work done in many and various directions by women.'

WI-HF_161 Essential war work: young ladies working as gardeners and assistants in the royal gardens at Windsor. Here they are tending chrysanthemums for the royal rooms and tables.

GWI-HF_160 Cornishwomen on the Prince of Wales's Duchy of Cornwall Estate at Princetown, on Dartmoor, are preparing sphagnum moss for use in surgical dressings. All the costs were met by the estate and the workers were volunteers.

GWI-HF_164 These two women are quenching coke in the retort-house. Such work was hot and grimy.

GWI-HF_162 The Midland Railway Company employed women in their goods department at Somers Town. Here they are seen loading and unloading heavy goods.

GWI-HF_163 'Coalies' of the Women's Legion, another voluntary body, are seen loading coal into sacks at a railway depot, prior to it being taken away on a lorry.

GWI-HF_165 As there was no male available to drive the fire engine, Miss Isobel Silver volunteered to drive the steam fire engine to the outbreak of fire at Blentworth Hall, near Horndean in Hampshire.

GWI-HF_167 A woman guard on the Metropolitan Railway. The original caption was both positive about the rôle and patronising at the same time. 'The Metropolitan Railway Company has not been slow to recognise the quick intelligence and reliability of women as guards, and similar officials on their service.' The 'photograph shows one of these unusual employees discharging her duties with ready intelligence.'

GWI-HF_166 Before 1917, London Zoo had been a male preserve. Here the first assistant lady curator is seen showing moths to children. Miss Cheeseman was in charge of three departments – water animals, butterflies and the aquaria.

GWI-HF_168 Chalk quarrying was another back-breaking job taken over by women.

GWI-HF_170 A further occasion when the caption writer was again both positive and condescending. 'It is not surprising to learn that "the Yellow Bird" (taxi) and its plucky driver are very popular and very much in request in Eastbourne, for Miss Scott has taken up her work in good earnest, and is a fully qualified and fully licensed taxi-driver. Those who know the comparatively small proportion of applicants who have been successful in qualifying for such a post in London can realise the satisfaction with which Miss Scott must have received her licence, and that she is well content with her work and popular with her clients is evident in our photograph. The conditions under which such work is carried out in Eastbourne differ largely from the more onerous nerve-trying conditions of London traffic, but none the less Miss Scott is to be congratulated upon her war-work.'

GWI-HF_169 A more sedate occupation was horticulture. These young women were on a six week 'war-training' course at Chester Horticultural College. The course was run at the nurseries of Messrs Dickson of Chester and included fruit and vegetable production and intensive culture.

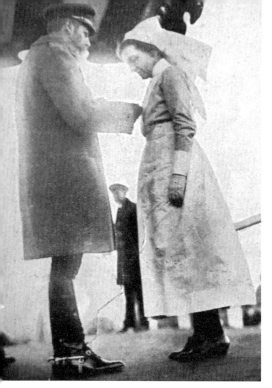

GWI-HF_173 Not only were women employed as nurses, they also drove the ambulances for London hospitals.

GWI-HF_171 King George is seen here presenting Nurse Emily Holmes with the Royal Red Cross Medal.

GWI-HF_174 Female employees servicing underground rolling stock at an unnamed depot.

GWI-HF_175 A similar scene in France: a female employee at work on an engine of the Paris Metro.

GWI-HF_176 In order to allow women with children the chance to work in the munitions factories, child-care had to be provided. This was often in the form of nurseries. Here Lady Rhondda (in front on the right) is opening a new nursery at Eridge House on the Fulham Park Road.

GWI-HF_172 A female gate-operator at work on the Bakerloo Tube Railway.

GWI-HF_179 Female lumberjacks at work in the forests of Brent Tor in Devon, producing pit props. Such work saved considerable shipping space, as previously the wood had come from Russia and Scandinavia.

GWI-HF_178 A young French woman who took over the role of a gendarme at Arques became known as 'The Belle of Arques'. Her duty was to control the barge traffic on the canal and the road traffic over the canal bridge. She is stopping a lorry before raising the bridge over the canal to allow a barge to pass.

GWI-HF_184 Another scene in France: women chimney-sweeps.

GWI-HF_185 Rheims was regularly bombarded throughout the war, but many people stayed in their homes. The population mostly lived in cellars under the wrecked houses but some shops opened daily and butchers and milk-sellers did daily rounds. In the illustration a milk-woman, neatly-aproned and wearing a possibly needed steel helmet, is taking round her morning milk.

GWI-HF_183 A female driver of an electric car in a French shrapnel factory that was used to transport materials to the various departments in the factory.

GWI-HF_181 A female tramcar driver in Bordeaux.

GWI-HF_182 French munitionettes checking shells in a munitions plant.

GWI-HF_186 In France women were employed as mechanics at training bases behind the front.

GWI-HF_180 Two Red Cross nurses attached to the Austrian Army in Vienna. They wore field-grey uniforms, with the Red Cross on their collars and caps.

GWI-HF_187 As in Britain, Austrian women replaced men as fire fighters. This is the fire brigade of a small town in the Austrian Tyrol: only six of the group are male.

Section 8
Wartime Life

GWI-HF_189 Examples of the shells made by the Cunard Shipping Company engineers.

GWI-HF_188 A photograph that clearly shows how well stocked British arsenals were in 1917. This is a northern ordnance factory during a visit by the Duke of Connaught.

GWI-HF_190 A happy Italian munitions worker standing next to 15-inch armour-piercing shells.

GWI-HF_194 American munitions plants increased their output rapidly after the declaration of war. This is a heavy plant at Bethlehem, Pennsylvania, where heavy guns, armoured turrets, and ammunition lifts were manufactured. The Bethlehem plant was the biggest of its kind in the world.

GWI-HF_191 A similar scene in Britain. The work area was kept very clean for safety, and because of a royal visitor. Each shell had to be clearly stencilled to show its size, type and date of manufacture.

GWI-HF_192 In the Toulon arsenal, workmen are varnishing shells externally and internally to reduce friction during the transport of loaded shells.

GWI-HF_193 Workers at a small-scale munitions factory in Beverley. Many small-scale producers like this made components rather than a finished article.

GWI-HF_197 Much munitions work was the manufacture of components that were sent to another factory for assembly. Here parts for aeroplane engines are being manufactured.

GWI-HF_195 On 23 April, the first battleship to be equipped with electric drive, a new form of propulsion, was launched. The USS New Mexico was 624 feet long, displaced 32,000 tons and was powered by oil.

GWI-HF_196 A similar scene on Clydeside but on a much smaller scale.

GWI-HF_200 The King and Queen, while inspecting a large munition works at Stockton-on-Tees, are pictured talking with some of the girl workers.

GWI-HF_198 The King and Queen on their visit to Hull.

GWI-HF_199 A photograph that clearly shows the structure of society. What possessed someone in authority to wear spurs when visiting an ordnance factory? Why could he not take off his own spurs? The spurs needed to be removed before entering an area containing explosives.

GWI-HF_201 During a visit to Bristol, the King talked to ten veterans who had fought either in the Crimea or in the Indian Mutiny.

GWI-HF_202 The popularity of visits by the King and Queen is clearly shown by this view of the crowds in Bristol.

GWI-HF_203 During a visit to a shipyard, the King talked to Martha Roxburgh. At just 14 she was the youngest employee.

GWI-HF_204 At the opposite end of the spectrum, he also talked to the oldest employee, an 84-year-old.

GWI-HF_205 Another view of life in Rheims: a knife-grinder with a steel helmet and gas mask.

GWI-HF_210 The Russian Revolution changed the balance of world power. These victims of the revolution are being buried at Tsarskoe Selo to a military march-past.

GWI-HF_209 In parallel with Britain in 1914, many American men volunteered to become special police. Once trained they wore a khaki, not blue, uniform, but, unlike in Britain, were armed with shotguns, revolvers and clubs to guard sensitive areas.

WI-HF_207 By 1917 anyone who wanted could be in a uniform of some sort. This young man is not a soldier, although he is wearing a soldier's uniform. He is in fact a member of the Red Cross.

GWI-HF_208 This older gentleman is a YMCA worker, although the uniform suggests otherwise.

GWI-HF_206 In the small part of Belgium that was not occupied, people tried to carry on with their lives. Here a Belgian soldier is watching an inhabitant making lace.

GWI-HF_212 With the Red Flag fixed to their bayonets, soldiers of the revolution are driven around Petrograd.

GWI-HF_213 The Tsar was held as a prisoner for a while at Tsarskoe Selo.

GWI-HF_211 Many British workers supported the ideals of the Russian Revolution. Two Labour MPs, Will Thorne and James O'Grady conveyed Labour's greetings to the Provisional Government.

GWI-HF_215 Delegates to the Workmen's and Soldiers' Council are seen holding a meeting in the Duma. They were appealing to their comrades at the front to fight for liberty.

GWI-HF_216 The Eagle Hut in the Strand was the headquarters of the American YMCA. It was, however, open to all Allied soldiers.

GWI-HF_214 A street scene in Petrograd during the revolution: Bolsheviks firing on the crowd.

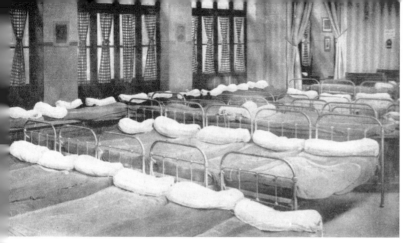

GWI-HF_217 Paris, like London, was the central terminus and departure point for troops. With hundreds of troops daily passing through, there was a need for sleeping accommodation. This picture shows night accommodation at the Gare de l'Est.

GWI-HF_218 Compare this with the above photograph of Parisian soldiers' accommodation. This is one of the bedrooms at the Church Army Soldiers' Hostel in Buckingham Palace Hotel in London.

GWI-HF_221 To celebrate Queen Mary's birthday on 28 May the branches of the Queen Mary Needlework Guild sent a 'shower of gifts' to her for the sailors and soldiers. 'Over one hundred thousand gifts of all kinds – games, pipes, walking-sticks, writing materials, blankets, etc. – were received by Queen Mary at St. James's Palace on behalf of the fighting forces.'

GWI-HF_219 The feeding arrangements at the Buckingham Palace Hotel.

GWI-HF_219a The military canteen at the Gare de l'Est.

GWI-HF_220 Soldiers required a wide array of goods not provided by the army. These were supplied by donations from the public. This shipment of footballs, games and books were provided by Japanese businessmen in London.

GWI-HF_224 Packing khaki-covered Bibles for the American Expeditionary Force and naval forces on active service. The Bibles were sent to YMCA depots near the front and to chaplains abroad.

GWI-HF_223 Lady Byron enlisted many helpers to provide socks for sailors and soldiers.

GWI-HF_222 A travelling canteen used by the YMCA to provide troops with tea and soup across London. It was presented by the London Warming and Ventilating Company and could boil 60 gallons of soup and 140 gallons of tea in two hours, using anthracite coal. The heating was carried out while the car is on the move.

GWI-HF_225 Queen Mary with some of the 102,000 birthday gifts sent to her.

GWI-HF_226 Realising that there was a shortage of stevedores, the government formed Transport Workers' battalions to help unload ships. Many dockers were immediately enlisted; they were allowed to live at home and told that they would not serve abroad. It was a clever way of calming potential unrest, as the soldier/dockers could not strike.

GWI-HF_227 The French had the same problem: a shortage of men. Here Territorial soldiers are carrying coal to coal merchants.

GWI-HF_228 Inland waterways increased in importance but as many of the men who worked the canals were in the army, the Royal Engineers formed special units to work the barges. Many of the men were former canal workers. They became instructors.

GWI-HF_229 The shortage of labour on the farm was solved by soldiers on furlough, convalescence or release. Here they are being trained to shear sheep.

GWI-HF_232 Alderman and Mrs Ball receive their son's VC from the King at Buckingham Palace during an awards ceremony.

GWI-HF_231 Four girl telephone operators who stuck to their work with courage and coolness during the progress of an air raid were awarded the OBE. The four were Miss Mabel Clarke, Miss Bertha Easter and Miss Lillian Bostock, who displayed great courage and devotion to duty during air raids; and Miss Florence Cass, who displayed great courage and devotion to duty while in charge of a telephone exchange during a serious explosion at a neighbouring munition works. The picture shows Miss Clarke at work.

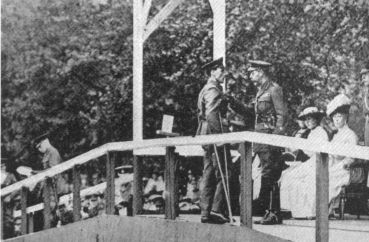

GWI-HF_233 Private Thomas Hughes, Connaught Rangers, receiving his VC from the King during an awards ceremony in Hyde Park.

GWI-HF_230 Many brave deeds were performed during the war, some of which were rewarded. Here a blinded ex-soldier is guided to the King to receive his bravery medal.

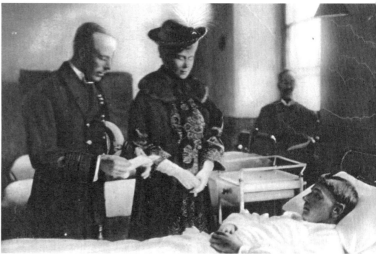

GWI-HF_235 On 9 May, Queen Mary, accompanied by Princess Mary, visited Haslar Naval hospital at Portsmouth. She visited several wards and presented Distinguished Service Medals to a number of men.

GWI-HF_236 During the royal visit to the north, the Queen is greeting the son of the late Captain Dunford DSO at the investiture at St. James's Park football ground in Newcastle.

GWI-HF_237 With growing shortages of staple foodstuffs, many took to growing their own. Lloyd George had a large vegetable patch which was supervised by his housekeeper. Here he is seen watching the weighing of some of his potatoes.

GWI-HF_238 The vicar of St. John's, Seven Kings, is seen with church volunteers creating an allotment in a public park.

GWI-HF_240 Everyone was gardening: here a group of sailors tend their vegetable patch at Scapa Flow.

GWI-HF_239 School boys released to help harvest the potato crop.

GWI-HF_241 The gardens of the Palace of Versailles and the Trianon were converted into vegetable plots. An Annamite soldier squad provided the labour.

GWI-HF_244 The explosion at Silvertown on 19 January rendered many people homeless. An official account said that 'three rows of small houses were practically demolished.'

GWI-HF_249 At St. Clement Danes, flower-girls are decorating the shrine before its unveiling on 9 July 1917 by Princess Beatrice.

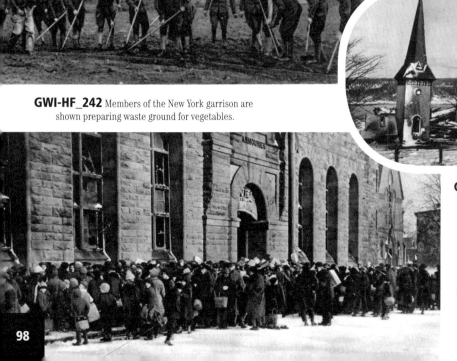

GWI-HF_242 Members of the New York garrison are shown preparing waste ground for vegetables.

GWI-HF_246 A poor-quality photo showing some of the extensive damage caused by the explosion on a munition ship at Halifax.

GWI-HF_245 An explosion at Halifax in Nova Scotia. This picture shows some of the many made homeless by an explosion at the harbour.

GWI-HF_247 The inauguration of a street shrine somewhere in the Hull area. Once common, most have now gone. Some listed those serving, some those who died, some did both.

GWI-HF_250 Princess Beatrice leaves the shrine after its unveiling.

GWI-HF_251
The first war shrine overseas was erected by the residents of Esquimalt, British Columbia and unveiled on 26 August 1917.

GWI-HF_252 As well as pictures of the wounded and dead, papers also published photographs of local men who had won medals for bravery. This is Lance Corporal James Eggleton of 48, Filey Road, Reading. He was awarded the DCM while serving with the 14th Battalion, Worcestershire Regiment.

Father and Brothers of Mrs. S. BRAZELL, Newsagent, Southampton Street Post Office, Reading.

GWI-HF_253 Papers also continued to publish pictorial accounts of patriotic families. This is the patriotic Gardner family from Reading.

GWI-HF_254 All mail leaving the country was checked for contraband, secret messages and news that was classified. The photograph shows the volume of confiscated mail by 1917. At that time a decision had still to be made about what to do with it.

GWI-HF_255 The famed Welbeck flower beds in Nottinghamshire were converted to growing market produce and tended by women land-workers.

GWI-HF_257 In 1917 a National War Museum was created to collect artefacts for posterity. This is a view of one room and its exhibits.

GWI-HF_258 A large portrait of Admiral Beatty being hung in the Allied exhibition of photographs of the war.

GWI-HF_256 In June 1917, the Postmaster General stated that his department dealt every week with nearly twenty million letters and parcels to and from members of the British fighting forces. Here men of the Royal Engineers are instructing women at the GPO in the sorting of letters addressed to men on military service.

GWI-HF_259 A prize exhibit at the new museum was the table used throughout the Somme campaign by Sir Douglas Haig.

GWI-HF_261 Queen Mary visited the National Welfare and Economy Exhibition on the first day. There were many stalls and displays. The purpose of the displays was to advocate economy in the purchase and use of the necessaries of life. Prices and food values of all articles were shown and practical demonstration given of ways to prepare them.

GWI-HF_262 The Lord Mayor's show went ahead as it had done in the previous war years. The procession included the Women's Land Army.

GWI-HF_263 A tank was part of the Lord Mayor's parade. It is seen here being directed by a policeman.

GWI-HF_267 Normal life continued as much as possible. What could be more normal than the Prime Minister speaking at the Welsh National Eisteddfod in Birkenhead?

GWI-HF_264 On 24 May 1915, Italy declared war on Austria. This is a view of the celebrations two years later when huge crowds gathered in Rome to hear patriotic speeches. There was a great procession to a house used as a hospital for wounded, and formerly occupied by the Austro-Hungarian Embassy to the Vatican.

101

GWI-HF_265 On Independence Day, the Mayor of Portsmouth, amidst the tumultuous cheering of a great crowd gathered in the Town Hall Square, hoisted the American flag between the White Ensign and the Union Jack.

GWI-HF_266 Parades were good for morale. These troops, passing St. Patrick's Cathedral, New York, were reviewed by Monsignor Lavelle, Vicar-General of New York and Rector of St. Patrick's. The 69th Regiment were leaving for mobilisation camp at Beeman, New York.

GWI-HF_270 Alfred Mason was charged with conspiracy to murder Lloyd George. (see photo 269 on following page)

GWI-HF_268 Yet another New York parade. A Red Cross demonstration marching down Fifth Avenue.

WI-HF_269 An important, and interesting case during the year was the conspiracy to murder the Prime Minister and Arthur Henderson, a Labour member of the Cabinet. The prison wardress is on the left with three of the accused: Hettie Weeldon, Winnie Mason, and Mrs Alice Wheeldon.

GWI-HF_271 The trial of the conspirators took place in the Guildhall at Derby. Alice was sentenced to ten years' penal servitude, Alfred to seven and Winnie to five. Hettie was acquitted.

GWI-HF_273 All the papers carried adverts like this.

NATIONAL SERVICE.

N.S.V. 26.

Occupation Classification Number.	Code Number of Office of Issue.	Volunteer's Enrolment Number.
44	1118	43802

Full Name of Volunteer _Charles John Kirk_

Address _78 E. Neville St_

This card should be carefully retained by the Volunteer. The three numbers entered above should be quoted by him in any communication relating to himself, in order that his case may be readily traced.

24 FEB 1917   Issued by _G. Wright_ _Nottingham_

on _the Welfy_ 1917.

C. Kirk

The Volunteer should sign here immediately on receipt of this card

(xs) (72507) Wt. G 23 100000 2-17 W B & L

GWI-HF_272 The government, in response to the shortage of labour, organised voluntary National Service whereby men and women worked for the war effort in a range of essential industries. Volunteers were to come from those not employed, that is, women, and those in non-essential industries. They would take up employment in essential industries. Volunteers were issued with a card like this.

GWI-HF_275 Echoing photo 83 on page 58, Reading Town Hall also flew the American Flag to mark the occasion.

GWI-HF_278 Not quite National Service but it made people feel they were contributing: war work in Bradford. The boys are making boxes for soldiers' parcels.

GWI-HF_274 Postcards were also used to highlight the service and make it more appealing.

GWI-HF_277 The other German aristocrat given a state funeral was the Duchess of Connaught, a full blood German Princess. This is her funeral procession: she had already been cremated so the coffin contained only an urn of her ashes.

GWI-HF_276 There were two royal state funerals during the year, both for German aristocracy. This is the state funeral of Prince Christian, a Danish-born German prince.

GWI-HF_280 Waste became valuable as shortages intensified. Women of the Red Cross ran a refuse-collecting department. Pictured are two Toronto based collectors of waste paper.

I-HF_279 When the second 'Liberty Loan' closed, a pyramid of historic wood was burned at Washington, the first of a national chain. It was lit using a candelabrum given by Napoleon to General Robert Pattison, who presented it to General Jackson on his inauguration as President. Among the historic relics burned 'were fagots from a cherry tree on the Mary Washington farm on the Rappahannock River, near a tree said to have been cut down by George Washington. There were also pieces of wood from the birthplaces of Presidents Wilson, Cleveland, Jackson, Johnson, and Polk. Illinois sent wood from Lincoln's old home; Missouri from Grant's log cabin; Arkansas part of the flagpole carried by Colonel Yell's regiment in the Mexican War; North Dakota, a shingle from General Custer's quarters at Fort Lincoln; Florida, a bit of the De Soto Oak at Tampa; and North Carolina, a piece of wood from Lower Cape Fear.'

GWI-HF_281 A by-product of converting coal to coke was coal gas. As there was a severe shortage of petrol for domestic use, many vehicles were converted to run on coal gas. The gas took up more space than petrol so a balloon was fitted on top to hold it.

GWI-HF_282 A commonplace occurrence by 1917: transporting a plane from the factory to its new base for checking and flight testing.

GWI-HF_284 Government had to continue so the House of Commons convened as normal. This is the modified version of the semi-state opening of the seventh session of the King's second Parliament.

GWI-HF_283 In order to conserve leather and streamline produ government- controlled factories began producing a high quali standardised boot for civilian use. Initially called 'standard boots' they officially became called 'Government controlled war-boots', but to their wearers they were simply 'war-boots'.

GWI-HF_286 Continuing a tradition, a Seaforth Highlander places a wreath to Scotland's national poet, Robert Burns, on his birthday, 25 January.

GWI-HF_287 There might have been a war on but all the same Reading continued its annual Children's Festival of music and drama: one of the acts in rehearsal – 'Tally-ho!'

GWI-HF_289 Men came home on leave, and some had a last photograph taken with their family.

GWI-HF_290 Even the sales continued. Quite where they managed
to get a surplus of stock from is an interesting question.

GWI-HF_291 Fashion was still important to many and somehow
shops managed to keep providing it, even when cloth was
at a premium. Paris was still the byword for fashion.

GWI-HF_292 The Royal Family continued with their normal duties throughout the war. Here they are marking Canada Day at Westminster Abbey.

GWI-HF_293 On St. George's Day, Queen Mary drove through Windsor and bought flowers wholesale for hospitals. Here she is accepting a bouquet from the Festival Committee. Even with a war on security was very lax.

GWI-HF_295 Unlike in Britain, any forcible resistance from this suspicious launch would have been met by a burst of machine gun fire.

GWI-HF_294 As in 1914 Britain and elsewhere, in 1917 America there was the possibility of spies and saboteurs. Anything suspicious was quickly dealt with. In this picture New York Harbour police have arrested suspicious characters from a barge.

GWI-HF_296 Like Britain, there were many pacifists in America. This photo was taken during a pacifist demonstration in Washington DC in April 1917, before the US joined the war.

GWI-HF 296a Inset: Another view of the pacifist demonstration.

GWI-HF_297 Fearing sabotage, bridges and public buildings were guarded. The Potomac River Bridge was guarded by regular troops.

GWI-HF_298 To boost the population and to combat poor health among the very weak was the aim of the first 'Baby Week' held in 1917. It was held across all four nations to highlight health care. There were numerous prizes. These are for the most beautiful baby.

GWI-HF_299 In order to highlight 'Baby Week', the borough of West Ham held a parade, headed by the ubiquitous Scouts movement.

GWI-HF_300 By 1917 Special Constables had been issued with full uniform, not just armbands. For those in cities and towns, the traditional helmet was often replaced by a steel helmet for safety during raids.

GWI-HF_303 In New York, Harbour police guarded the docks and ships and the NYPD guarded the outside of the docks. The photograph shows the locked area where German liners were interned.

GWI-HF_304 Echoing picture 280 on page 105, Toronto waste collectors, this is an ad from a local paper asking people to sell their waste paper.

GWI-HF_304a A shop display in the War Economy Centre of the Citizen's Committee in Birmingham highlighting the necessity to prevent waste.

GWI-HF_305 The same message, this time in Keighley, which had the 'enviable fame…of reducing their bread consumption well below that of the voluntary allowance.'

GWI-HF_306 There were spies in America but not all were tried there. Bolo Pasha, a Frenchman by birth, was a German agent. He is pictured here (second from left) leaving the Palais de Justice in Paris after interrogation after his return from America where the authorities had managed to find evidence for his conviction. He was arrested in Paris on 29 September 1917, charged with treason, and tried at court martial. Pasha was executed by firing squad on the morning of 17 April 1918 in Vincennes.

GWI-HF_307 The war continued to impinge on the rights of neutral nations. If they did not want their ship to be attacked it had to be painted in red and white vertical stripes.

GWI-HF_308 There were food shortages in Holland as well. This is a food demonstration in Amsterdam.

GWI-HF_310 With navigational aids in their infancy, it was not unknown for planes to land at the wrong aerodrome or even on the wrong side. This German fighter landed at Aardenburg in July 1917.

GWI-HF_309 Dutch citizens in Britain had bought Westgate House as an officers' convalescent home and, on 3 March, Mme Van Rappard and a party of Dutch nurses passed through London on their way to the Western Front. The country was neutral but obviously many of the citizens were not.

GWI-HF_311 There were riots in Madrid and martial law was imposed. As a result the army gave a show of strength to prevent any 'excesses on the part of riotous sections of the civilian population'. This is an infantry picket with machine gun near the Ronda de Atocha in the southern quarter.

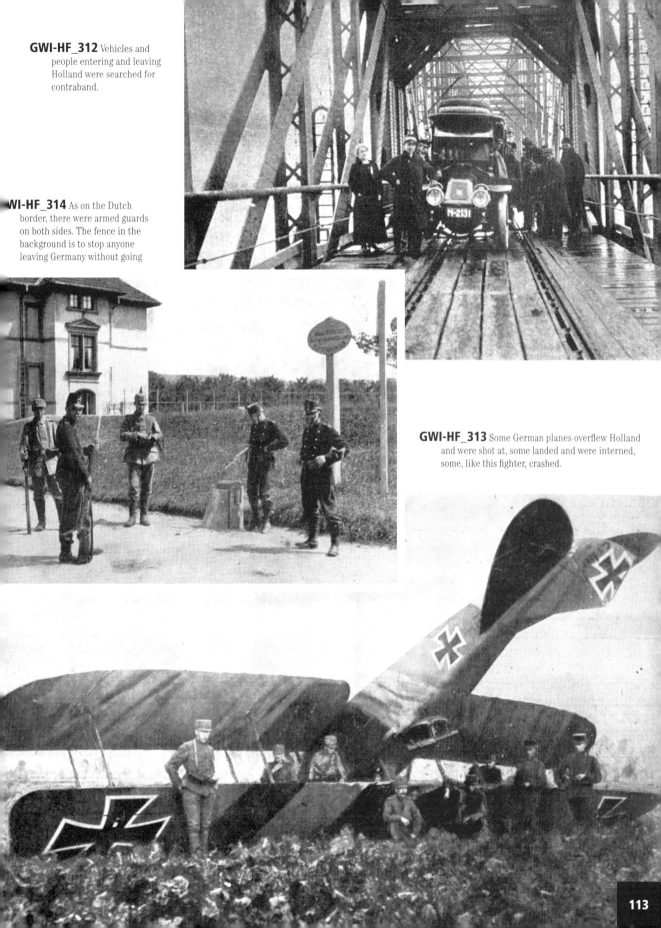

GWI-HF_312 Vehicles and people entering and leaving Holland were searched for contraband.

WI-HF_314 As on the Dutch border, there were armed guards on both sides. The fence in the background is to stop anyone leaving Germany without going

GWI-HF_313 Some German planes overflew Holland and were shot at, some landed and were interned, some, like this fighter, crashed.

GWI-HF_315 To help with the food shortages, Holland adopted rationing, like the warring nations. Here they are preparing bread cards for each inhabitant.

GWI-HF_316 A similar scene but in the Camberwell Food Control Office where they are preparing sugar cards to ensure an equal distribution.

GWI-HF_317 There are differences in this photo to photos 315 and 316;: there are boys and girls helping out, and it is in France. Every country had problems with food supplies.

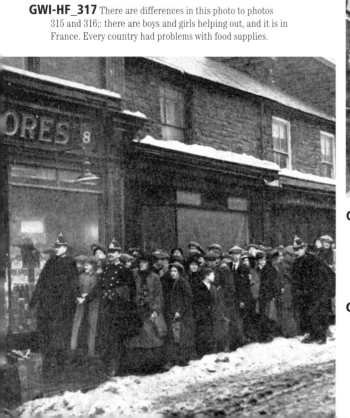

GWI-HF_318 This queue for potatoes is in Hoxton during the winter of 191 17. The mayor had procured three tons for the poor of the borough with th distribution being controlled by the local police.

GWI-HF_319 The queue was a new concept but quickly became ubiquitous. This is a butter queue at Tonypandy in present-day Mid-Glamorgan during the winter of 1917.

GWI-HF_320 Food economy was paramount because of shortages; reducing waste to a minimum was essential. In St. John's Wood, boys and girls were taught simple cooking; the simple meals they made were then taken from house to house in the neighbourhood in which the kitchen had been established. This saved the householders time and money and provided a nutritious meal.

GWI-HF_322 Food waste was taken seriously by all. Schools had a Food Control Court where offenders were tried, and fined if guilty.

GWI-HF_321 There were severe penalties for hoarding food: confiscation and fines. This haul came from one household.

GWI-HF_323 Young boys looking at the menu in the Women's Dining Room at a war-controlled factory. The menu was designed to both appeal and to be nutritious. Communal eating saved scarce resources.

GWI-HF_329 The purchase of bread, sugar and meat all needed cards in some areas before a national scheme was developed. Here in Birmingham Council House, 900,000 meat cards are being prepared for distribution.

GWI-HF_328 There wer queues for just about everything by the end of the year. The front of Smithfield Market was usually covered by rows of carcasses but by 1917 meat was in short supply. This is the queue for the joint of meat for the Sunday roast in late 1917.

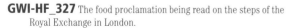

GWI-HF_327 The food proclamation being read on the steps of the Royal Exchange in London.

GWI-HF_330 Apart from areas where there were already ration cards, many people undertook a voluntary food pledge: 'I realise that economy in the use of all food and the checking of all waste helps my country to complete victory, and I promise to do all in my power to assist this campaign for national safety.' Shown here are patriotic Londoners at Grosvenor House signing the pledge.

WI-HF_331 Along with allotment cultivation, the waste land along railway lines was turned into vegetable plots. The London & Southwest Railway provided seed potatoes to employees who wanted to cultivate this waste land.

GWI-HF_332 With winter drawing in, low supplies of coal meant looking for alternatives: wood & peat were obvious answers where they were available. Here customers in Paris are attempting to haggle over a purchase of wood.

GWI-HF_334 Parisians, like Londoners, were short of coal: the queue for the small amount carried by such a merchant's rully.

GWI-HF_336 Throughout the war money was collected for a range of good causes. The six ambulances illustrated were presented to the Red Cross by the Scottish mine workers and inspected by the King before the photograph was taken.

GWI-HF_339 Helena Schilizzi, the wife of Elefthérios Venizélos, one of the most significant figures in Modern Greek history, paid for this field operating theatre.

GWI-HF_338 Publicity was essential to raise money for War Bonds. The pigeon is about to despatch an application for £250,000 to the Tank Bank in Trafalgar Square.

GWI-HF_337 Harry Lauder was a patriot who did yeoman service throughout the war for the Allied cause, even though he lost his son in France. Here he is seen addressing New Yorkers outside the Sub-Treasury, New York, on behalf of the Liberty Loan.

GWI-HF_340 A pageant was a good way to raise money for to the war. This is a 'Liberty Loan' procession marching through Wall Street to raise money.

GWI-HF_341 Parading captured U-boats was also used to gain attention and stimulate 'Liberty Loans'. The captured submarine UC5 parade was viewed by thousands.

GWI-HF_343 Some of the ladies who were at work and not looking after the home or queueing for coal: Post Office workers in Nottingham.

GWI-HF_344 Fund raising in Japan: a tea-concert at a hotel in Tokyo in aid of distressed Belgians.

GWI-HF_348 Towns and cities tried many ways to increase War Bond purchases. Scarborough wanted a real submarine to moor in the harbour as a bank during Business Men's Week to stimulate the purchase of War Bonds. There was no submarine available so

GWI-HF_345 The tank was a novel way of raising money. Known as Tank Banks, they toured the country encouraging people to invest in War Bonds. In this picture a cheque for £20,000 is being handed over to invest in War Bonds for King George's Fund for Sailors. On the tank are sailors, all of whom had been in torpedoed ships.

GWI-HF_346 Tank 113 is shown arriving in Holborn to collect the Prudential's investment of £628,000, interest on £25,000,000 already invested by the company in the War Loan.

GWI-HF_347 Tanks were also used in America to get the public to invest in government loans. This tank, pictured in New York, was used in the five billion dollar Liberty Loan. It was part of a 100,000-person parade along Fifth Avenue.

GWI-HF_349 Children were also encouraged to save to help the war effort. The pupils of Friern Barnet School are waiting, with their savings book, to hand over their money.

GWI-HF_351 Some collections were for local causes. This clock showed how much money had been collected in the Reading area towards the 'Berkshire Room' at the Star and Garter Home for severely disabled soldiers and sailors in Richmond.

WI-HF_350 There were Flag Days throughout the war, so many that they had to be booked in advance and follow a strict protocol. Shown are just four of the many types of flag sold in a year. Three are self-explanatory; the one bottom left was sold to raise funds for the Russian Red Cross.

GWI-HF_353 Animals we[re] good for getting small change out of people, especially in bars. Spot, the Vine Hotel, a public house in Reading, had raised £33, mostly in halfpennies, for various charities when this pho[to] was taken.

GWI-HF_355 A subtle reminder that the War B[onds] was finishing. This is on [the] base of Nelson's Column

GWI-HF_352 Reading set a target of £2,000,000 in war loans and established a bureau to boost investment. A barometer was regularly updated to show how much had been saved. When this photograph was taken there was still a long way to go.

GWI-HF_354 A large advertising board on a public building encouraging people to buy War Bonds.

Section 9
Christmas

GWI-HF_356 It was the fourth Christmas of the war. New flags have been added to this Home Front Christmas card but one would not be there for the final war Christmas.

GWI-HF_357 Following a centuries-old Christmas tradition, the better-off gave to those not as fortunate. These are just some of the parcels distributed by the Reading Philanthropic Institution. What was in the parcels the newspaper did not record.

GWI-HF_358 A German Christmas postcard: 'Emperor and nation thank the army and navy.'

GWI-HF_359 A Christmas card sent by an officer at Craiglockhart hospital in Edinburgh. The cover is apt, yet the name and verse would have meant little to most. Craiglockhart was a specialist centre for shell-shock.

GWI-HF_360
Men from the Cambrai battle making Christmas decorations in a London Hospital.

GWI-HF_361
Christmas is the season of giving. These were gifts only the better-off could give.

WAR IS WASTE, BUT MANY CHRISTMAS PRESENTS

are wasteful too. Only the useful Present is justified in times like these. Fortunately "Kendall" Umbrellas are useful as well as beautiful; as Presents they are ideal. Thousands to choose from, but choose early at

KENDALLS, Umbrella Experts,
21, BROAD ST., READING.

GWI-HF_362 A clever advert linking in with the national waste reduction drive.

GWI-HF_363 Sergeant Kelly was ready for Christmas when the situation in Italy changed and a number of British battalions were sent to reinforce the Italians. This would probably have been the first his family knew of his change of address.

ON CHRISTMAS DAY
AS USUAL

You are kindly asked to take up a Collection for the Lord Roberts Memorial Workshops

THE

National Tribute to Lord Roberts

LAST year the Organiser of the Tribute Fund originated a Dinner Table Collection to help to build and equip the Workshops. The idea of asking the Public to take up this collection was to involve the Fund in as little expense as possible and thus each sum sent went in full to the Fund. Envelopes were supplied last year and these are available again this year if you will kindly write to us for as many as you need. Your guests will be glad to fill the Envelopes and will enjoy their Christmas Dinner all the more because they have helped many Soldiers and Sailors whose bravery and sacrifice made the Dinner possible.

THE £500,000 National Tribute Fund is now more than half completed thanks to the generosity of thousands of people who loved the late Field Marshal. It is hoped to complete the Fund very soon now. When this is done the Workshops will be self-supporting. You are asked to visit the Workshops and see the men happily at work once more after all but losing their lives for you. The more you investigate the methods of the Workshops and the handling of the Fund the more you will give. We invite the fullest inspection of every detail of our work for the wounded men.

Christmas Day Collection Envelopes
ARE NOW READY
Please send for yours to-day

Please send Donations and Applications for Envelopes to Lord Roberts Memorial Headquarters, 122, Brompton Road, London, S.W. 1. Please make Cheques payable to

| GIVE ALL YOU CAN THIS CHRISTMAS TO OUR FUND. | Major-Gen. Lord Cheylesmore, K.C.V.O., CHAIRMAN. Major Tudor Craig, Comptroller. Charles Frederick Higham, Honorary Appeal Organiser. | GIVE 'ALL YOU CAN THIS CHRISTMAS TO OUR FUND. |

GWI-HF_364 Giving was not just about presents. The Lord Roberts Memorial Workshops provided men with employment and were funded solely by donations. At Christmas householders were asked to give an envelope to each guest for them to contribute. The envelopes were later collected.

GWI-HF_365 A War Bond was an ideal gift for all ages.

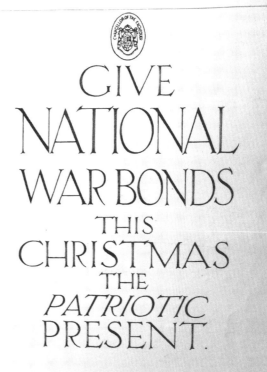

GIVE
NATIONAL
WAR BONDS
THIS
CHRISTMAS
THE
PATRIOTIC
PRESENT.

Bonds for £5, £20 and £50 can be bought at any Money Order Post Office or most Banks. You can buy as many as you like. All you have to do is to sign the application form at the Post Office or the Bank with your own name " for and on behalf of " the person to whom you wish to make the present. You will then obtain a Bond Book made out in the recipient's name, with the amount of the Bond entered up in it, which you will post off or otherwise present with your Christmas wishes. Be sure and give War Bonds this Christmas.

GWI-HF_366 Like their British counterparts, Australian soldiers also sent Christmas cards home. As mail took weeks to get to Australia, the card would have been sent quite a long time before Christmas, and for some families it would arrive, possibly with a cheerful message inside, after a telegram informing them that their son/husband was wounded or even dead.

Wishing you the Compliments of the Season

CANADIAN ENGINEERS

C. E. T. D.

ST. JOHNS
P.Q.

December, 1917

GWI-HF_367 A card from a Canadian
soldier to the folks at home.

GWI-HF_368 After Christmas came New
Year's Eve, a time to have a party and dress
up. This woman is probably subconsciously
echoing the hopes of the Allies: the arrival
of the Americans in force could help end
the war.

1917 Home Front Timeline

January

1   RFP up 3 per cent since December, Rail fares up 50 per cent over 1916 price. Wheldon family arrested for plot to murder PM on golf course with poison dart fired from air rifle – jailed in March. The official films *Battle of the Ancre* and *Advance of the Tanks* are released.

5   WAAC formed.

8   Start of a two-day strike of munitionettes in Leeds over the dismissal of a girl for striking a forewoman.

10 Marguerite Francillard, a spy for the Germans, executed at Vincennes.

11 Terms of new war loan announced – 5 per cent interest, issue price 95 and principal repayable in 1947 or 4 per cent interest, free of income tax, issue price 100 with principal repayable in 1942. Important food orders issued by Lord Devonport: millers had to increase the amount of flour extracted by additional milling (5 per cent) or to add other cereals (up to 10 per cent); the use of wheat except for seed and flour forbidden. The same orders fixed the price for chocolates and other sweetmeats.

12 French government fixes the price of butter.

16 General Lawson's report recommends official employment of women with the army in France.

17 To end Paris munitions strike, French government sets a minimum wage.

19 Explosion at Silvertown, East London – 69 killed and 450 injured – heard in Salisbury.

20 French Supply Ministry closes bakeries for two days a week. In Britain the Military Service Act removes all exemptions for men under the age of 31.

23 Labour Party approves acceptance of office by Labour members. The RNAS bomb blast furnaces near Saarbrücken.

25 Southwold on the Suffolk coast shelled at night by enemy vessel – no casualties. In France restaurants are restricted to only two courses.

26 Compulsory loan or sale to Treasury of certain foreign securities.

30 Age of call-up in Britain increased from 18 to 18 and seven months.

31 Germany declares unrestricted naval warfare to all neutral states within the war zone. German submarines will sink both combatant and neutral shipping at sight from 1 February. Nearly 35,000 British troops are involved in munitions work.

February

1   Constantinople University proposes Kaiser for the Nobel Peace Prize. In Germany the production of both steel and gunpowder drop. Unrestricted U-boat war begins. German daylight bomber offensive against Britain (Turkenkreuz) is postponed due to shortages.
2   Lord Devonport appeals to the nation for voluntary food economy. During the month, meat consumption falls by 15 per cent.
3   President Wilson severs diplomatic relations between USA and Germany.
5   The National Service volunteer scheme begins enrolling 18 to 61-year-olds.
6   New Air Board formed under Lord Cowdray. Mr Chamberlain announces new scheme for National Service.
7   American citizens taken hostage in Germany. Strikes in Moscow and Petrograd. Private motoring almost eliminated when petrol licences are withdrawn.
9   Denmark rations sugar.
12 In Britain a 4lb loaf of bread now costs 11d.
13 Mata Hari arrested in Paris.
15 British Government takes over all coal mines in the UK for the period of the war.
16 False air raid alarm in London when airship LZ107 overflies Deal after bombing Calais. Food production to be boosted by availability of 30,000 troops for farm work.
17 New war loan estimated to reach over £700 million. Government to revise exemption certificates for men under 31.
20 Price of *The Times* doubles to 2d.
    New British blockade orders – vessels sailing to and from neutral countries, which have access to the enemy, must put into a British port for examination, or be liable to capture.
22 Dutch ships, with safe passage guaranteed by German government, sailing near Falmouth are attacked by submarine U3 – four sunk.

23 In Ireland, twenty-eight Sinn Fein members are arrested and exiled for alleged plotting with Germans. The PM warns of further import restrictions, announces minimum oat and wheat prices through to 1922 and a minimum wage of 25s a week in agriculture.
25 New war loan subscriptions amount to £1,000,312,950. Broadstairs and Margate bombarded for ten minutes by Germans causing slight damage. Three people killed and one wounded.
26 British government requisitions Dutch ships in British ports.

March

1 Air raid on Kent – six injured. RFP up 3 per cent to 92 per cent. France rations sugar. Mlle Dufays, a munitions worker, shot for selling secrets to the Germans.
2 French call up the 1918 class.
3 15,000 women volunteer for National Service in three days.
5 A shortage of potatoes is forecast. Consumption of meat in London falls from 31,600 tons in January to 23,450 tons in February.
7 Recruiting for WAAC (Women's Auxiliary Army Corps) temporarily completed with 114,803 enrolling for National Service.
8 A speech by Sir Edward Carson spells out the dangers of food shortages if the German naval threat is not stopped. There would be further restrictions as 500,000 tons of food had been sunk in February. Over 100,000 have volunteered for the National Service scheme.
9 Lord Devonport sanctions maximum food prices.
12 Russian Revolution begins – Provisional Government formed. In Britain a new Bread Order makes sale by weight compulsory.
13 British government takes over all quarries and mines (non-coal).
15 Vote of credit in House of Commons. Tsar Nicholas abdicates.
16 Acute potato famine in England and sugar supply stands at 40 per cent of 1915 level. Zeppelin raid on Kent and Sussex – no casualties. German aeroplanes over Westgate – no casualties. Albert Hall meeting in favour of National Service for women. Four R-class Zeppelins raid France. L39 shot down by AA fire.
17 Aeroplane raid near Dover – no casualties.
18 Ramsgate and Broadstairs shelled by the German destroyers – no casualties.

19 Eight-hour day legalised. Mr Bonar Law announced that the cost of the war was now £6 million a day for the financial year to 31 March 1917. However, over six weeks it had cost £7 million a day. The National Debt now stands at £3,900,000,000.

21 German decree partitions Belgium into French speaking Wallonia and Flemish speaking Flanders. Tsar arrested.

22 German Interior Minister tells the Reichstag that infant mortality is lower than in peace time, general national health is surprisingly good and that the food restrictions are not serious.

23 Zeppelins bomb the island of Mudros.

20 Ministry of National Service formed. Shortage of petrol and coal.

25 Decision taken to send Bolsheviks in Switzerland back to Russia in a special train.

26 Mr Bonar Law appeals to engineers on strike at Barrow to resume work. Price of bread rises to one shilling for a 4lb loaf and a new standard of flour is applied to bakers.

28 Mr Asquith announces his conversion to women's suffrage. Women's Army Auxiliary Corps formed.

29 Speech by Mr Bonar Law says 100,000 more men are needed. Military Service (review of exemptions) Bill is passed.

31 Order limiting output of beer in United Kingdom issued. Only nine weeks' wheat and grain supply in the country.

April

1 British government decides to intervene in the Barrow Engineers strike. British shipping losses at highest since the start of the war.

2 Government gives Barrow strikers twenty-four hours to resume work.

3 Barrow strike over.

4 Hotels, boarding houses, clubs and restaurants subject to food orders – a weekly meatless day, five potato-less days, 3½ lbs of bread, 14 ounces of flour and ½ lb of sugar per person. Flour order increases the amount of non-wheat flour in bread. TUC told the army needs 500,000 more men by July

5 Aeroplane raid on Ramsgate – no casualties. Men previously rejected for military service and some invalided out of the services to be re-examined.

6   USA declares war on Germany. Food hoarding order – prohibits anyone from buying more than the household actually needs and for dealers to sell food where there is reason to believe that the amount of food allowed will be exceeded; houses can be searched if owners thought to be hoarding food.

7   Cuba and Panama declare war on Germany.

9   Munitionettes pay raised to 24-27s a week.

10 To improve the coal situation, 40,000 miners released from the German army for work in the mines.

13 Board of Trade asks farmers to limit use of human foodstuffs in fattening cattle and feeding horses not doing productive work.

14 A meat shortage in France results in two meatless days a week.

15 Rioters in the Brazilian town Porto Alegre burn about 300 German buildings over two days.

16 Food orders – prices of wheat (78/- for 120 lbs), barley (65/- for 100 lbs) and oats (55/- for 78lbs). Barley to be requisitioned by the Food Controller (other than home grown and not kiln dried). A cut in the German bread ration results in large-scale strikes in Berlin and Leipzig.

17 The King visits Sopwith Aviation Company.

18 Food order restricting pastry and cake making.

19 Speech by Herbert Fisher, Minister of Education, on educational reform and the desire by the government for people to be good citizens. This was to cost around £40 million.

20 Germans shell Dover and neighbourhood – no casualties.

21 Any Berlin strikers refusing to return to work to be drafted immediately. In Britain, to supply the needs of the army, all doctors of military age are called up.

23 Plans to convert 3,000,000 acres of grassland for sowing in 1918; schoolboys urged to work the land.

25 Corn Production Bill intended to increase the amount of arable land and guarantee minimum prices to farmers and minimum wages to labourers. Call-up of doctors stopped.

26 German Naval raid on Ramsgate, Broadstairs and neighbourhood on the night of 26/27 – 2 killed and 3 injured.

30 Jockey Club decides to stop racing after 4 May. Tonnage of Allied and neutral shipping lost in April is the worst in the war (also not exceeded in second war). Under ten days' sugar supply, and potato crop of 1916 almost finished.

May

1   New schedule of Protected Occupations; agriculture protected. Under new scheme very few men, and those only in very special circumstances, who are classified A and B1 will be able to escape military service. RFP up 4 per cent to 98 per cent. A National War Museum announced in the Commons: later became the Imperial War Museum.

2   Further Food Orders extend the powers of the Food Controller. Budget announced – no new taxes but tobacco duty and entertainment tax increased. Government estimates war expenditure as £2,290,000,000 with a revenue of £639 million. In America, the 1st Liberty Loan for $2 billion raises $3 billion from just 4 million people.

3   British Trade Corporation founded with capital of £10 million.

4   Food situation in Germany worsening. At Crefeld PoW camp, the guard is doubled to stop locals raiding the inmates' Red Cross food parcels.

5   Flat racing discontinued as the public were strongly opposed to racing in the present climate of events. Also the severe restrictions on oats made further sport impossible.

6   Royal Proclamation read out in church for four consecutive Sundays urging people to eat 25 per cent less bread. First night aeroplane raid on London, between Holloway and Hackney. The five bombs dropped cause three casualties.

8   U-boat rammed and sunk in the Thames estuary.

10   Unofficial strikes by 160,000 engineers against dilution of private work.

11   Daylight aeroplane raid on NE London, 1 killed and 2 wounded. In Paris, 10,000 clothing workers strike against the cost of living.

12   Combing-out of munitions workers begins. The closing of bakers in the Lisbon area caused food riots. Over 200 killed and martial law declared.

13   Daily expenditure on the war now £5,600,000. Vote of credit for £500 million demanded in Parliament. Two new groups of attestation, 41 to 45 and 45 to 50.

14   King George tours industrial centres in the North. Labour unrest – London buses and engineers go on strike and weavers in the north threaten to strike.

15   Due to the political situation in Russia, the Russian flag day in Britain was not very successful, with many refusing to buy.

16   Lloyd George proposes Home Rule in Ireland at once.

18   Unit of USA Medical Corps reaches England. Selective Conscription Act enacted in America for men aged 21 to 31.

19   Settlement with Amalgamated Society of Engineers agreed upon.

20   Conscription announced in Canada.
21   Imperial War Graves Commission chartered.
23   Four Zeppelins raid Essex, Norfolk and Suffolk – 3 killed and 16 injured.
24   Unofficial engineering strikes stop after strike leaders released.
25   Failing to reach London, Gotha bombers raid Kent and Folkestone – 95 killed and 192 injured (more than in any Zeppelin raid); three raiders brought down.
27   Due to a shortage of paper, ink and workers, an estimated 600 German newspapers have closed since the start of the war.
29   Mr Arthur Henderson goes to Russia on special mission.
31   Meat Sale Order published. Bread consumption during the month is 10 per cent less than February.

June

1   Lord Devonport resigns as Food Controller. Labour party appoints deputation to Stockholm and Petrograd. Police arrest British agents with leaflets for Germany in Switzerland.
3   Socialist conference at Leeds.
5   Daylight aeroplane raid, by twenty-two Gotha bombers, on Thames estuary and Medway – 13 killed and 34 injured in Shoeburyness and Sheerness; four machines destroyed while returning. Draft Registration Day for 10 million American men aged 21 to 31. An estimated 3,000 men fled to Mexico. While Labour Party members were demonstrating in Trafalgar Square for the world's industrial workers, Sinn Feiners were rioting in Dublin.
11   Sailors' and Firemen's Union refuse to let Ramsay MacDonald and other delegates sail for Russia.
13   Serious explosion in munitions factory at Ashton-under-Lyne kills 41. Daylight aeroplane raid on London, Margate and Essex by 14 Gotha bombers – 162 killed and 432 injured, including 46 children in Poplar School. In Toulouse, 5,000 female ammunition workers strike with red flags for higher pay.
15   Release of Irish rebels announced. Lord Rhondda appointed as Food Controller.
16   Two hundred die during a smallpox epidemic in northern Germany. British release remaining Easter Rising prisoners after Dublin demonstration for their release.
17   Two Zeppelins raid Kent and Suffolk – 3 killed and 16 injured. One Raider, L48, downed after suffering double engine failure and attacks by three RFC planes.

18   British pensioners in special hardship to get a supplementary allowance of up to 10s a week.

19   Peerages conferred on the Battenberg and Teck families. The King abolishes the British Royal Family's claim to German hereditary titles. The Commons votes to give wives over 30 the vote.

21   Warrant instituting 'Order of the British Empire' published.

25   First American troops arrive in England.

27   Martial law declared in Spain.

30   To ease the coal shortage, 50,000 troops are released for mining.

July

1   RFP up 2 per cent to 103 per cent.

2   The King and Queen attend service at Westminster Abbey for jubilee of Canadian Federation. Greece declares war on the Central Powers. During race riots in St. Louis, 37 Black Americans are killed. In New York, 15,000 blacks stage a silent protest march.

3   Summer holidays limited to one week by the Ministry of Munitions.

4   General Pershing leads 14,500 American troops through Paris.

5   Aeroplane raid on Harwich and Suffolk – 17 killed and 30 injured.

6   50,000 metal workers in Cologne strike for higher pay and 51-hour week.

7   Big aeroplane raid on London and Margate – 57 killed and 193 injured; 11 enemy aeroplanes accounted for. Anti-foreigner riots in the East End.

9   Secret session of House of Commons on London air raids. The battleship HMS *Vanguard* blows up at Scapa Flow with 843 fatalities. RNAS bomb the War Ministry in Constantinople and the battleship *Goeben*.

11   Sinn Fein candidate defeats Nationalist in East Clare election.

13   Deputation on London Air Defences received by the Prime Minister.

14   First Bastille Day parade in Paris since 1914.

15   In neutral Dutch waters, the RN capture four German steamers and force two more aground on the Dutch coast.

17   Royal proclamation changing name of Royal House and family from Saxe-Coburg-Gotha to Windsor. Changes to the government announced, including Winston Churchill becoming Minister of Munitions.

20   Government decides to lower bread and meat prices; loaf now 3d cheaper, compared to March price of 1s.

22 Aeroplane raid on Essex and Suffolk – 13 killed and 26 injured. Siam declares war on Germany and Austria-Hungary. Start of National Baby Week to nurture infant life and reduce early death.

23 Amendment to Corn Production Bill defeated; minimum agricultural wage to be raised to 30/- a week instead of the 25/- proposed in the original bill.

24 Vote of Credit for £650 million moved. Recruiting system to be transferred from War Office control to the Local Government board. The trial of Mata Hari begins in Paris.

25 Irish Convention opens with Sir Horace Plunket in the chair. At New Ulm in Minnesota, 10,000 attend an anti-draft rally.

27 Ramsay MacDonald's motion to approve the Reichstag Peace Resolution of 19 July defeated by 148 to 19 votes. Soviet meeting in the East End broken up.

August

1 RFP for August falls 2 per cent to 102 per cent. Last death sentence passed on a German spy – later commuted.

2 Led by anarchist stokers, 600 men of the German battleship *Prinzregent Luitpold,* idle in Wilhelmshaven for nine months, stage a mass walkout about meagre rations and draconian punishment.

4 The King and Queen attend special service at Westminster Abbey for third anniversary of the war. At Invergordon a force of 3,000 Russian troops arrive for service on the Western Front.

8 German night-fighters shoot down first Allied night bomber near Frankfurt-am-Rhein.

10 Labour Party Conference decides by large majority to send delegates to the Socialist conference in Stockholm.

12 Aeroplane raid on Essex and Margate – 32 killed and 46 injured; two raiders downed.

13 Bonar Law announces that no passports will be issued for travel to the Stockholm conference. China declares war on Germany and Austria. In Britain the maximum price for cereal is fixed until June 1918.

14 American troops pass through London on their way to the front; Stars and Stripes and Union Jack flown side by side from the House of Commons.

18 Government forbids threatened strike by the Associated Society of Engineers and Firemen.

20   Food shortages in Hungary cause release of all civil prisoners serving sentences of under two years. Swiss agree to export 200,000 tons of coal and 19,000 tons of iron to Germany.

21   Labour Party reaffirms their decision to send delegates to Stockholm. Zeppelin raid on East Yorkshire – one injured. One Zeppelin brought down off Jutland. Ministry of Reconstruction formed.

22   Last daylight raid on England, against Dover, Ramsgate and Margate – 12 killed and 25 injured; three raiders brought down. A bread shortage in Turin led to a factory close-down because of a strike. The ensuing riot saw shops being sacked and two churches being burned down. To clear the streets, the army was called and used tanks and machine guns. Order was restored with 50 deaths and 800 arrests.

22   The King and Queen visit Canadian wounded at Taplow. After a white policeman hits a black woman, black soldiers at Camp Logan, near Houston, riot – 17 deaths.

29   Demonstration in Montreal against conscription.

September

1   RFP up 5 per cent to 106 per cent. Government provide free air raid damage compensation.

2   Aeroplane raid on Dover – 1 killed and 6 injured. Trades Union Congress at Blackpool partly settles Stockholm Programme but with much opposition.

3   Six German aeroplanes bomb Sheerness area – 132 killed and 96 injured, mostly naval ratings.

4   German submarine fires 30 shells at Scarborough – 3 killed and 6 injured. Gotha bomber raid on London and the south-east counties – 19 killed and 71 injured; one plane destroyed by AA fire. TUC declares against Stockholm Conference by overwhelming majority. Edmund Dene Morel sent to prison by Winston Churchill for distributing anti-war literature in Ireland. In 1924 he defeated Churchill for a seat in Parliament. He was nominated for the Nobel Peace Prize in the 1930s.

8   Price of milk fixed for three months after October at 8d per quart.

11   First party of repatriated British prisoners of war arrives from Switzerland.

13   Martial law proclaimed in Portugal to stop a general strike.

14   Sugar rationing begins in Britain.

17   Nine-penny Loaf Order in force. Count Luxburg affair. Daily flat rate wage of miners increased by 1s 6d.

18 Sir Arthur Yapp becomes Food Controller.

22 German War Office orders factory shutdowns because of serious coal shortage. French bombers raid Frankfurt, Koblenz, Stuttgart and Trier.

24 Aeroplane raid on London, Kent and Essex – 21 killed and 70 injured. Only two of the twenty-four planes penetrate the London defences.

25 South-east London raided by German aeroplanes – 9 killed and 23 injured. Zeppelin raid on Yorkshire and Lincolnshire coasts – 3 injured.

26 In the previous week, 75 strikes reported in Britain.

27 National War Bonds (5 per cent and 4 per cent, latter free of income tax) started.

28 Aeroplane raid on the Home Counties; raiders headed off from London with no damage. Bolo Pasha arrested in Paris as a German agent.

29 Aeroplane raid on London. Three machines penetrate the defences – 14 killed and 87 injured.

30 Aeroplane raid on London. Four machines penetrate the defences – 14 killed and 38 injured. Trade union unemployment over 1 per cent - highest since June 1915.

October

1   Due to the bread subsidy, RFP falls 9 per cent to 97 per cent. Aeroplane raid on Essex, Kent and London – 11 killed and 41 injured. First of ten proposed London balloon barrages becomes operational.

2   Five per cent National War Bond issued. Britain declares an embargo on exports with Holland and Scandinavia to prevent goods being re-exported to Germany.

3   Sugar ration in France reduced to 18oz a month and bread rationed in towns over 20,000.

7   Poorest harvest in France for fifty years.

9   American government authorises the formation of an all-black division, with white officers. It is accepted as a combat unit by the French Army.

11 Government stops commercial cable communication with Holland. After the Formation of 41 Wing, RFC, the British launch a 13-month daylight bombing offensive against industrial targets, up to 125 miles from the Western Front aerodromes, in Germany and Alsace-Lorraine.

12 Count Luxburg is interned in Argentina. The Japanese offer of 2,000 doctors to replace GPs in the army is rejected.

13 Engineers and moulders working for the Ministry of Munitions receive a 12½ per cent bonus.

15 Bonar Law announces future Air Ministry Bill. Mata Hari shot as a spy.

17 For dropping insulting leaflets over Germany, two RFC officers sentenced to ten years in prison.

19 Thirteen Zeppelins raid the Midlands, Eastern Counties and London – 36 killed and 55 injured. Five machines brought down.

21 German Treasury Minister tells War Office that financially a continuation of the war is not viable.

23 New York police prevent a plot for a 1918 Easter Rising by Sinn Feiners.

24 Franco-British convention for military service allows French nationals in the UK and British nationals in France to be drafted for military service. Sinn Fein hold convention in Dublin. RNAS again attack in the Saarbrücken area.

25 Italian PM and cabinet resign. The Sinn Fein conference in Dublin elects De Valera President and announces the Irish Republic constitution.

26 Brazil declares war on Germany two days after interning forty-three German merchant ships, allegedly over Germans caught in a plot to invade the country.

27 Suffrage parade in New York.

29 Attempted air raid on Essex driven off. Parliament's thanks voted to Navy and Army.

31 Aeroplane raid on Kent and Dover – no damage. Further raid on Kent, Essex and London – 10 killed and 22 injured. A government recruitment statement says that, by the end of October, 4,421,694 men had enlisted.

November

1 RFP now 106 per cent. In America, farm prices up 31 per cent on 1916 prices. Recruiting taken over by the Ministry of National Service. Coal rationing starts. Taxi fares rise by 75 per cent for the first mile. In Constantinople now three meatless days a week.

2 Balfour Declaration.

5 Butter prices fixed for all brands. Railway wage increased.

6 New York State grants women the vote.

8 Arrival in London of USA mission under Colonel House. Bolsheviks seize power in Petrograd.

9 Lord Mayor's Banquet. Unskilled munitions workers demand 12 per cent bonus.

10   Air Force Act sets up new government department – the Air Council with a Secretary of State at its head and a status similar to the Admiralty and Army Council.

12   New scale of voluntary rations introduced; meat was limited to 2lb, butter and fats to 10oz, sugar to 8oz and bread 3½lb to 8lb per head per week, according to sex and occupation.

15   Reds win control of the Kremlin. In Ireland, hunger strikers are released. To save energy, the American fuel administrator bans electric signs on Sundays and Thursdays.

16   Brazilian capital and six states in a state of siege. Police in Brazil arrest 700 enemy aliens, mostly German reservists.

18   Rumours that Russia will shortly withdraw from the war.

19   Bolsheviks call for an armistice on all fronts. Britain stops cement exports to Holland.

20   The Commons disenfranchises conscientious objectors. Food position serious in France and Italy due to harvest failures.

22   A 12 per cent bonus is given to 500,000 unskilled munition workers.

23   All class distinctions and civil ranks abolished in Russia. The church bells in Britain ring to celebrate the victory at Cambrai.

25   In the last free election in Russia until 1989, the Socialists beat the Bolsheviks. In Budapest, 100,000 workers march for peace, and in support of the Russian Revolution.

26   Aircraft workers in Coventry successfully strike and gain recognition for their shop stewards. The 3rd French war loan opens and raises 10.2 billion francs.

27   Doctor Elsie Inglis dies on her return with the Scottish Women's Hospitals from Russia. The British Trading with the Enemy Act is extended to enemy aliens interned in neutral countries and the buying of foreign currency and shares is forbidden. The alcohol content of beer in America is reduced to 3 per cent.

29   Germany accepts Lenin's offer of an armistice. Women's Royal Naval Service set up under Katherine Furse.

30   Coventry aircraft works on strike with 50,000 men and women idle.

December

4 In America War Savings and Thrift stamps go on sale. Compulsory food rationing begins in Rome and a voluntary food ration scale is issued to all under 18s in Britain. The Saint Etienne munitions factory is closed by a strike. Four German PoWs briefly escape from Farnborough.

5 The democratic government of Portugal is overthrown by Major Paes and 1,500 soldiers. French form the independent Czech Army. The US Trade Board blacklist 1,600 German firms working in Central and South America.

6 Raid by 25 aeroplanes (Gothas and Giants) on Essex, Kent and London – 8 killed and 28 injured. Two of the raiders are brought down. Finland declares Independence. American government ends the manacling of conscientious objectors. Munition ship explosion in Halifax, Nova Scotia, levels two square miles, causing 2,682 casualties, leaving 25,000 homeless.

7 America declares war on Austria-Hungary.

10 Panama declares war on Austria-Hungary.

11 Balfour announces receipt in September of German peace proposals. Non-Ferrous Metals Bill passed.

12 Railway disaster in France: a train jumps the tracks, 643 killed.

16 Cuba declares war on Austria-Hungary.

17 In Russia all church property to be confiscated and religious teaching to be abolished. Postal restrictions to neutral countries announced by British government.

18 Aeroplane raid on London, Essex and Kent – 14 killed and 85 injured. Captain Murlis-Green is the first night-fighter pilot to shoot down an enemy aircraft. Congress approves prohibition.

20 Australia rejects conscription.

21 Local food rationing authorised in Britain.

22 Lord Rhonda's scheme for rationing by localities comes into force. Bad weather stops Gotha raid.

27 Brazil enacts conscription for 21 to 30 year olds.

28 Austrians bomb Padua causing 70 casualties.

29 First trainload of badly wounded British PoWs arrives in Holland for internment.

31 Lord Rhondda issues model rationing scheme. Italian government told the country only has thirteen days' food supply. Total British air raid casualties for the year – 697 killed and 1,644 injured.

Bibliography, Sources and Further Reading

Baer, C.H. *Der Völkerkreig*, Volumes 18 to 25. Julius Hoffmann, 1917/18.

Barnett, M. *British Food Policy during the First World War*. Allen & Unwin, 1985.

Becker, J. *The Great War and the French People*. Berg, 1990.

Bilton, D. *Hull in the Great War*. Pen & Sword, 2015.

Bilton, D. *Reading in the Great War*. Pen & Sword, 2015.

Bilton, D. *The Home Front in the Great War – Aspects of Conflict*. Leo Cooper, 2003.

Charman, I. *The Great War, The People's Story*. Random House, 2014.

Chickering, R. *Imperial Germany and the Great War, 1914-1918*. Cambridge University Press, 2005.

Connor, J., Stanley, P., Yule, P. *The War at Home*. Oxford, 2015.

Fridenson, P. (ed.) *The French Home Front, 1914-1918*. Berg, 1992.

Gregory, A. *The Last Great War, British Society and the First World War*. Cambridge University Press, 2008.

Hastings, M. *Catastrophe*. William Collins, 2013.

Herwig, H.H. *The First World War. Germany and Austria-Hungary 1914-1918*. Arnold, 1997.

Horn, P. *Rural Life in England in the First World War*. Gill & Macmillan, 1984.

Kennedy, R. *The Children's War*. Palgrave Macmillan, 2014.

Kocka, J. *Facing Total War, German Society 1914-1918*. Berg, 1984.

Markham, J. *Keep the Home Fires Burning*. Highgate Publications, 1988

Martin, C. *English Life in the First World War*. Wayland, 1974.

Marwick, A. *The Deluge, British Society and the First World War*. Macmillan, 1973.

Marwick, A. *Women at War*. Fontana, 1977.

McGrandle, L. *The Cost of Living in Britain*. Wayland, 1974.

Reetz, W. *Eine ganze welt gegen uns*. Ullstein, 1934.

Rex, H. *Der Weltkrieg in seiner rauhen Wirklichkeit*. Hermann Rutz, 1926.

Robb, G. *British Culture and the First World War*. Palgrave, 2002.

The Berkshire Chronicle.

The Hull Times.

The Hull Daily Mail.

The Reading Standard.

Turner, E.S. *Dear Old Blighty*. Michael Joseph, 1980.

Unknown. *Großer Bilder Atlas des Weltkrieges*. Bruckemann, 1917.

Unknown. *History of the War*, Volume 13. The Times, 1917.

Unknown. *History of the War*, Volume 14. The Times, 1917.

Unknown. *The Illustrated War News*. Illustrated London News and Sketch, Ltd., 1917.

Unknown. *Illustrated London News*. January–December 1917. Illustrated London News and Sketch Ltd., 1917.

Unknown. *Kamerad in Westen*. Societäts-verlag/Frankfurt am Main, 1930.

Various. *Thuringen im und nach dem Weltkrieg*. Lippold, 1920.

Williams, J. *The Home Fronts*. Constable & Co Ltd, 1972.

Winter, J. M. *The Experience of World War I*. Equinox (Oxford) Ltd, 1986.

Winter, J. *The First World War*, Volume III Civil Society. Cambridge University Press, 2014.

Wilson, H.W. (Ed.) *The Great War, The Standard History of the All Europe Conflict*, Volumes 6 to 8. Amalgamated Press, 1916.

Index